What oth_._ _._ _.._ _.,_._ _

From The Mom's Corner

"My greatest accomplishments in life have been to raise and nurture my four bright, creative and talented daughters. I am honored to have been asked to contribute to this wonderful book.
Thank you for this opportunity." - **Deborah Flynn**

"I love this – my kids will love this." **- Charlie Whittamore – Travel Agent**

"What an excellent book – I find myself reading it when my life gets out of balance and in a short time I'm usually calm and back on track. It keeps me focused on the best things in life." - **Tom Adkins – Marketing Director**

"This book is remarkable – I thoroughly enjoyed it and often read excerpts from time to time." **Donna Watson – Computer Analyst**

"This book is a great reference book on life. I keep it out all the time for my kids to see, read, and be inspired." **Dorothy Walthers – Health Ministries**

"This is one of the greatest gifts I could give to my sons." **– Sara Horn – Mother**

"This is great. Every Mother and Father should be writing a page to their children." **– Chip Whitehouse – Retail Manager**

"This book is so moving and catches a mother's love. It's inspiring and a joy to read." **– Rachel McDonough – Elementary Teacher**

What others are saying about
From The Mom's Corner

"I feel honored that I was given the opportunity to contribute to such an awesome book!" **Cathy Blatnik**

"Thank you for this amazingly powerful book – filled with lots of wonderful emotions. I love it." **Vicky Thompson – Real Estate Agent**

"I wish I had a page from my own mother." – **Tom Hattersfield – General Contractor / Field Division**

"This book is so awe-inspiring and influential that I'm giving one to each of my own children." – **Shirley McDermitt – Science Professor**

"This book shares a glimpse of the immense power of a mother's love. " - **Karen Wojciechowski**

"I am honored to be included in such an incredible and heartfelt project. It is a gift not only for a child but also for a mom to tell her story and share her thoughts and lessons." -**Joann Ward - Registered Nurse**

"Raising children is often challenging and they seldom want to hear what I have to say. They seem to listen to other mothers more than me. I continue to encourage my children to read this book and others like it because it helps to instill good values. As a loving parent I want all the help I can get to keep my kids on the right track." **Anonymous**

From The Mom's Corner

More than 60 outstanding mothers share with their own sons and daughters their deepest and most intimate thoughts on life's lessons.

R. K. Ketterer

Publisher
From The Dad's Corner
Alexandria, KY

From The Mom's Corner

From The Dad's Corner Publishing
19 Spillman Drive
Alexandria, KY 41001

ISBN - Soft Cover 978-0-9881875-1-1

Printed in the United States of America

Library of Congress Control Number: 2013954764

A THOUGHT FROM THE MOM'S CORNER

"I realized when you look at your mother, you are looking at the purest love you will ever know."

Mitch Albom

About the Author

The author of *From The Mom's Corner* (and *From The Dad's Corner*) is a single father who raised two beautiful daughters.

Attended: University of Wisconsin, University of Kentucky, Northern Kentucky University, Ohio College of Applied Science. Bachelor of Science – Business Management

35 years as a corporate manager in telecommunications

Producer of award-winning cable television show –
Entertainers in the Tri-State
25 nominations – 14 awards in
Cultural Awareness – Diversity – Community Action –
Entertainment – Documentary – Performing Arts

Producer – *Stars of Magic* production

Motivational Speaker, Author, Real Estate investor, and Entertainer/Magician

A word from the Author

Why Write This Book?

Shortly after my daughter's wedding in 2011, I decided to write a letter directly to both of my daughters.

I wanted to echo and reiterate the values that I tried to instill in them, and guide them as they were growing up. I wanted to make sure that my life's experiences and words of encouragement and wisdom were always available to them.

This letter was another way to reach them: a way to assure that my children don't miss any important messages about life; just another way to share my feelings with them; to let them know that I love them and that I am proud of them.

Soon many fathers wanted to join in and write to their own children. This gathering of ideas was the impetus that was to become a whole book of fathers' wisdom, *From The Dad's Corner*. Within 5 months, 60 outstanding fathers from 9 different states and 4 countries, from many walks of life, with more than 3,500 accumulated years of experience had shared their treasure trove of their deepest and most personal thoughts and wisdom about life's lessons with their own children. This first book was the springboard for this second companion book, *From The Mom's Corner.*

The fathers' pages are absolutely outstanding: full of great information, wisdom, guidance, experiences and emotion: sharing Life's Lessons about Balance - Finance - Relationships - Work Ethics - Friends - Family - God - Attitude - Failure - Motivation - Goals - Choices - Education - Time - Success -and many more.

From The Dad's Corner and now *From The Mom's Corner* are inspirational and powerful books about life. They promote parents to be more involved and encourage young maturing adults to set goals, make good decisions, and stay on the right track. They act as a compass and a beacon in life, giving direction and showing the way while reinforcing the need to keep God in one's life.

In compiling this sequel, *From The Mom's Corner*, I have been blessed to talk with many brilliant and dedicated mothers throughout the U.S. and other countries. The essence of this second book is a mother's love.

The attributes of the second book are very much the same as *From The Dad's Corner* but with an extra dose of love and emotions.

The mothers and fathers did not always share the same priorities or points of view. However, many common elements of love and concern, between the two viewpoints, quickly emerged.

Good fathers and good mothers are not trying to keep their children from growing up even though they may express themselves differently. Actually what they want is very basic – they want their children to experience a good life – one better than they had. They want their children to live a balanced life, being self-assured, and being triumphant in their pursuits.   They want them to have meaningful, long-term relationships and have good morals and ethics throughout their lives. Parents just want their children to live healthy, happy, and rewarding lives.

So over 120 good parents, in these two books, have come together to allow the readers to peek into their private thoughts and words, words that they share with their own children. They are talking to their own children – not to you – not to me - and we are permitted to listen in and be enlightened by these conversations. These pages from the fathers and mothers may also help minimize some of life's difficulties, problems, and heartaches. Essentially, our children and the readers of these books are presented with many insights and values that focus on the blessings that enrich our lives.

I continue to encourage my daughters, Robin and Katie, (and you – the reader) to keep these two books readily available to read – to refer to them often, especially when their (your) lives get out of balance. These two reference books are the truest information available about living, about life, about living a good life.

A THOUGHT FROM THE MOM'S CORNER
"The mother-child relationship is paradoxical and, in a sense, tragic. It requires the most intense love on the mother's side, yet this very love must help the child grow away from the mother, and to become fully independent." <div align="right">**Erich Fromm**</div>

DEDICATION

As the author, I would like to dedicate this book to the five most important people in my life.

To:
My parents- Charles Ketterer (now deceased) and Alice – who have carried out a lifelong commitment to being dedicated parents and who both have lived by an incredible work ethic, which they have instilled in their five children.

My daughters- Robin (Ketterer) Quallick and Katie (Ketterer) Scarlato – who have taught me more about life than I could ever teach them. They have allowed me to enjoy the wonderful blessings and endure the difficult challenges that come with being a father. They have inspired this second book as well as my first book *From The Dad's Corner*.

My dearest friend- Regina Katherine Hellyer – who is my significant other; she has enriched my life in so many ways, brought me happiness, has taken me to new heights and taught me how to enjoy life.

A THOUGHT FROM THE MOM'S CORNER
"My mother is my root, my foundation. She planted the seed that I base my life on, and that is the belief that the ability to achieve starts in your mind."   *Michael Jordan*

ACKNOWLEDGMENTS

This second book project is a sequel to my first – From The Dad's Corner and both have quickly grown to include many different people throughout the U.S. and other countries. It became an intense labor of commitment and took the combined efforts of many to accomplish this remarkable book. I wish to acknowledge the following:

Regina Katherine Hellyer
For her endless typing, transcribing, editing; her patience with me as I focused on this time consuming and powerful project; and her encouragement through the challenging times.

63 Outstanding Mothers
For taking their time to gather their thoughts and submit wonderful pages and for being willing to share their deepest ideas and experiences on life's lessons.

Katie Scarlato (nee Ketterer)
For designing the front and back covers of this book as well as my first book – *From The Dad's Corner.*

A THOUGHT FROM THE MOM'S CORNER
"Knowledge is, in the end, based on acknowledgement."   *Ludwig Wittgenstein*

TABLE OF CONTENTS

FORWARD

By Regina Hellyer / English Professor

We are all familiar with the joke about mothers having eyes in the backs of their heads. Ask any child with a loving mother and you will realize that there is a lot of truth to that idea!

Erma Bombeck describes God's dilemma in creating a devoted and ever-vigilant mother this way:

> One pair [of eyes] that sees through closed doors when she asks, 'What are you kids doing in there?' when she already knows. Another here in the back of her head that sees what she shouldn't but what she has to know, and, of course, the ones here in front that can look at a child when he goofs up and say. 'I understand and I love you' without so much as uttering a word. [Excerpt from the poem "When God Created Mothers"]

The imagery of a loving mother's awareness is more than amusing: It is a beautiful metaphor for a mother's watchful and loving protection of her children.

Our mothers guide us as kids--sometimes more closely than we desire. They instill individuality and confidence in us as teens when we cautiously enter the grown-up world. Then, as adults, our devoted mothers give us the praise, freedom, and encouragement that we need to find our own way; they give us wings to fly.

Of course, mothers are not perfect, but good mothers help shape our personalities and values in ways that no other relationship can. Her job description is long, detailed, and very challenging, but in reality she is a key player in the bigger picture: "God can't be everywhere so He created mothers."

Enjoy this book of cumulative wisdom from over 60 mothers. They are among the many dedicated, loving mothers who have stepped up to the plate and risen to the challenge. Their calling is a high and sacred one, and they have answered the call with utmost love and devotion.

A THOUGHT FROM THE MOM'S CORNER

"... there had been the two little boys. Now they were gone, too. They loved her and called her and sent her e-mails and would still snuggle up to her to be petted when they were in the mood, but they were men, and though they would always be at the center of her life, she was no longer at the center of theirs."

Cathleen Schine,
The Three Weismanns of Westport

INTRODUCTION

The essence of this book is to capture a mother's love. It is certainly an impossible task, but hopefully we come close by giving more than 60 outstanding and wonderful moms the opportunity to share their deepest thoughts and emotions by writing to their own sons and daughters.

It is the truest and most relevant information available about life. In a world of technology where we can retrieve an enormous amount of information at the click of a mouse or by the touch of a finger, we instantly become inundated with particulars on any subject we ponder. The problem we now face is sifting through all this information, trying to sort out what is pertinent and true and what is not.

There is no greater compilation of truth because good parents typically live and breathe for the betterment of their children.

This book provides over 60 wonderful, intelligent mothers with the opportunity to communicate and share their thoughts. It gives them a voice – a record of their words.

In the pages that follow, you will be exposed to the wisdom, the values, the guidance, the perceptions, experiences and advice that are shared by various outstanding mothers in many different walks of life.

It's advice that many good mothers are giving to their own sons or daughters. It's an accumulation of more than 3,400 years of experience. Along with *From The Dad's Corner*, it's the single collection of the truest and most openhearted information available to pass on to you and to generations to come.

Catherine B.

Catherine B.
Born: Washington, DC
BS: University of Maryland
Stay-at-home wife and mother
Married 17 years to Lawrence B.
Three children:
Stepson - 29
Daughter – 16
Son - 8

Best talent: Baking, cooking, blogging and taking care of my family and friends the best I can!

To my children,

CLB (stepson) –

From the very first time that you and I met over 22 years ago, I knew that I wanted to be your stepmom. One of the happiest days of my life was when I married your dad and I "officially" became your stepmother. I have watched you graduate from high school, college and graduate school. You have worked hard at your career and I am super proud of you. I hear of stepchildren and stepmothers not getting along. I'm so glad that you and I don't fit into that category!! Our closeness and love for each other is greatly treasured by me, and I don't ever take it for granted. I feel blessed that you came as part of the "package" when I married your dad. I'm honored to be called your stepmom. I have and always will support you. All my love, Cathy

LCB (daughter) –

My dear, sweet (and only) daughter, I can remember when you first went to preschool over 12 years ago. It was one of the hardest things for me because I knew it was just the beginning of you starting on that road to independence. When you were in second or third grade and you told me you weren't going to call me "mommy" anymore, I knew you were taking another step towards independence. I was so happy and proud when you read your speech at your eighth grade graduation, knowing that high school was just around the corner. When you got behind the wheel of the car for the first time, I knew it was another step on that "road" to independence. Now, as your senior year of high school looms in the very near future, I know that our relationship will continue to change and I am okay with that. You have matured into a beautiful young woman inside and out, and I can't wait to see what the future holds for you. All my love, Mom

DMB (son)

To my "baby,"

When I found out that I was pregnant at age 40 with you, I knew even before the doctor told me that you were a boy. Finding out that you had Autism at age 2 ½ was unexpected. You have had more challenges than other kids, but you continue to amaze us with how much you learn every day. I know in my heart of hearts that you were given to us for a reason. You teach me and everyone else that knows you what unconditional love really is. My hope for your future is that you will graduate from high school and college and one day have a family of your own. For now, I am grateful that you are still small enough to fit onto my lap and give me hugs and kisses.

Love,
Mommy

A THOUGHT FROM THE MOM'S CORNER
"Biology is the least of what makes someone a mother." **Oprah Winfrey**

Colleen Bolton

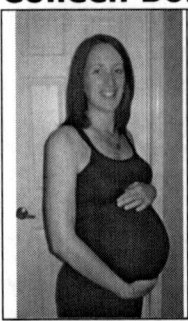

Colleen Bolton
Born 1981 - Married to Gregg for 4 years
2003 – Postgraduate Certificate in Primary Education, University of Edinburgh, Scotland
2002 – Bachelor of Arts, Sociology, University of Guelph, Ontario
CAREER - Teacher
HOBBIES – Cooking, hiking, camping, canoeing

To my daughters, Hannah Mary (age 20 months) and Evelyn Irene (age 2 months),

Know that: This is being written in the middle of the night as I feed my new baby girl, Evelyn. Despite the challenges of these early newborn days, I am convinced that motherhood is and will be the most important role I will play in my life. While I am still learning how to be better as a mother and wife every day, know that I will do everything in my power, with your father, to give you the opportunities to live life to the fullest.

The top values I encourage for you are:

COMPASSION AND EMPATHY FOR OTHERS
We are fortunate to live the life that we do, in this country, and in our home, and it is important to recognize how fortunate we are. From our educational opportunities, to access to plentiful food and clean water, it is important to take the time to reflect on our many fortunes in life and not to waste the opportunities we have been presented with.

CREATE YOUR OWN DEFINITION OF SUCCESS
Attempt to stray from the traditional path of what our society deems as success. Wealth will buy you many aesthetic things, but it will not buy you true friendship or relationships built on trust, loyalty and kindness. Success shouldn't be measured by the number of degrees hanging

on your wall, dollar signs in your bank account, or clothes in your closet. Take the time to travel and explore our world, until you find what it is in life that makes you feel fulfilled and happy, and ultimately successful.

LOVE THE ONE YOU'RE WITH

I feel truly blessed to have met your father in university, and we have been supporting each other's goals and passions since those early days. While we share a lot of commonalities, we continue to challenge each other every day by expressing our differences of opinions in a respectful way. I love you girls as much as I do, because I have a partner who is fully committed to the same aspirations for our life together as a family. Find someone that makes you laugh, supports you when you're down, and ultimately brings happiness to all aspects of your life.

All My Love,
Mom

A THOUGHT FROM THE MOM'S CORNER

"Mothers observe all, absorb all, give all, forgive all, offer all, suffer all, feel all, heal all, hope for all, and pray for all. But most of all, Mothers *love always*."

Richelle E. Goodrich

Linda Bowers

Linda Bowers
Graduated from Eastern KY University with Masters in Education / Taught physical Education / Married to John Bowers since 1972 / Attends Alexandria United Methodist for 63 years / Hobbies are Going to Bible study, playing volleyball and mah jongg, and doing watercolor paintings.

To my three children – Jami, Seth, Sara, their spouses (between the ages of 31 and 35), and my eight grandchildren,

Know that: Wow, when I was asked to share my feelings on motherhood many thoughts came to mind. I thought of how many roles a mother fills. We have to be a shuttle driver, fix-it person, cleaning lady, dishwasher, laundry maid, nurse, teacher, preacher, caregiver, but most of all a loving wife and mother.

I do many things in love for you. I need to let you know that I will always love you unconditionally, listen to you, and always be here for you.

I pray for you without ceasing. I started praying for you, and us as parents, before you were born and have never stopped praying.

As you know, your dad and I have been married for forty-one years. We have three children, and eight grandchildren. We are very involved in all of your lives – babysitting, going to church together, going to dancing recitals, athletic events, vacationing, eating out etc. I believe a family that prays together stays together.

The top values that I encourage for you are:

ATTENDING CHURCH
I believe that you and we all need to grow up attending church, with the parents, and hopefully give your life to Christ.

ROLE MODELS
Parents and grandparents need to be good role models for their children and grandchildren. I think it is good for children to see their parents hugging and kissing and enjoying laughing with each other.

DISCIPLINE
When children do wrong, I believe they need to be lovingly disciplined with consistency. As the Bible says, "Train up a child in the way he should go and when he grows older he shall not depart from it."

I love being your mother and grandmother, and I take my role seriously.

Sandy Dean Adams Broering

Sandy Dean Adams Broering
Graduate: Knott County Central High School
and University of Louisville
Physical Therapist, practiced in a variety of
settings for 20 years, honored to have met
many great people
Hobbies: family time, UK basketball fan,
running, hiking, reading, tossing baseball
with my sons, photography, and gardening

To my sons, Bryce (16), Braxton (12), Braydon (3),

Know that: I love you! Being a mom means I get to be
blessed 3 times, to laugh a lot, to learn much, to love
more deeply, to give thanks for each year I witness you
each grow. God's character shines through our growth as
a family and I appreciate each stage. I have realized my
weaknesses and strengths. I am more compassionate,
courageous, and composed. My destiny was confirmed
with each son and my journey is abounding with each of
you.

FAITH
Be courageous. Accept His gift to you. Life has
difficulties and those often make us stronger once on the
other side. God promises to be with you through the
storms. He may not change your circumstances, but He
can change your heart/ perspective. Be an over-comer.
Be tenacious about pursuing God's direction and love.

LOVE
Be wholehearted. Give love and receive it as God
designed each of you. Always remember that each of you
is worthy of being loved. Set boundaries with others. Be
kind to those younger. Be patient with those older. Be
generous with your time, especially with those you love.
Children are a blessing from God. I have 3! God shows
the design for love through a family. My story began with

a mother's love. I love you more than anything... in the whole world. My favorite thing is being your mom.

HOPE
Be compassionate. Serve others. Stay connected with family and friends. Be a good husband and father if your path leads you there. Seek God's ways. Praise and worship at church and in everyday life. Together, find peace that passes all understanding amidst the storms.

TRUTH
Be truthful: To yourself and others. Don't rely on your own understanding: Look in the Word. Acknowledge Him in your ways and He will direct your path. Let your light shine! You each are meant for amazing things. Be merciful and don't judge. You can't know what it's like to walk in another's life. Temptations lure us when we are too hungry, angry, tired, or lonely.

JOY
Be healthy. Eat right and sleep regularly. Exercise daily. Stay in control of your emotions so that you can handle problems well. Be happy. Smile a lot. Breathe deeply. Take a vacation. Work earnestly. Play passionately. My joys are seeing you, which make my heart lighter, receiving your gracious hugs and kisses, and laughing with you because we know funny things happen to me.

With that said... Be thankful. I am thankful for the opportunity to be part of 3 great men. Remember John 3:16. Follow the B's. Enjoy each other. Blessings and love to each of you!

ILU! Mom

Susie Clark

Mary Sue (Susie) Birkenhauer Clark
Married to Stanley Allen Clark for 38 years.
More in love now than the day we were married!
Have four (4) great children, Carrie, Kyle, Christopher and Courtney
Have six (6) wonderful grandchildren, Adyson, Reagan, Jackson, Carter, Kenzie and Presley
Have worked for the City of Alexandria for 18 years. It's a great job!

To my children, Carrie, Kyle, Christopher, and Courtney, (between the ages of 29 and 35),

Know that: I am so happy at your strong sense of family. You are truly happy for one another when you succeed. There isn't any jealousy among you, only love. You are all so giving. Remember, God will never be outdone in generosity, for only what we give away, enriches us from day to day! You all love to have everyone over to grill out or just hang out. That's so important.

The top values I encourage for you are:

CONTENTMENT
Dad has always said, "BE CONTENT WITH WHAT YOU HAVE." I certainly think these are words to live by. Always be thankful for what you have. Material things will never make you happy and I think you all know that.

SERVICE
Always remember we are here to serve one another. We are never too good to serve; service to others truly makes you happy. Don't be quick to judge others. You don't know what's happening in their lives to make them behave the way they are behaving. Be patient with others.

PARENTING

I want you each to know what amazing parents I think you are. You take so much time with your children and have so much patience with them. You are very unselfish parents and that's important. Your parenting skills show through your children, my grandchildren. They are so loving and well-mannered and hilarious children.

GROWTH

Continue to grow and experience new things. Take on challenges and bloom where you are planted! No matter what comes your way, always remember: "I don't know what my future holds, but I know who holds it," and "Jesus come quickly; I need you." He'll never let you down!

You are the best family I could ever have asked for or imagined. I love you with all my heart and I pray for you daily.

All my love,

Mom

A THOUGHT FROM THE MOM'S CORNER
"No one in the world can take the place of your mother. Right or wrong, from her viewpoint you are always right. She may scold you for little things, but never for the big ones. "
Harry Truman

Mary Ramirez Cook

Mary Ramirez Cook
Born in 1961 in Cincinnati.
Mother of 5
Dance instructor and owner of
A-Marika Dance Company
Founder and President of
A-Marika DS

To my five gifts from God:
Rick, Jorge, Erika, Tony and Mathew,

Know that: From the minute I knew about you, my heart was yours. I never once had anything but excitement and love for the new life that was being entrusted to me. Even though most of you are now grown, you still have my heart and will always be the loves of my life.

The top values I encourage for you are:

GOD
Place your trust in God's hands. He is there for you and will always listen to you. He knows what is best for you and will help you get through life's difficult times. You don't have to be in a church to live with God in your heart. You may experience doubt, but don't give up. God will never leave you. We all have a guardian angel. We may not always see them the way we saw Mathew's, but we each have one who will be with us during the darkest times. Believe!

FAMILY
I do feel I have successfully taught you the importance of family. I am so thankful when I see all of you together. The laughter, the crying, the helping one another and even the fighting makes me see the love you have for

each other. Your family will always be there for you: through good times and bad. You are so blessed to have each other. Please never forget that and keep that family value strong for your children. You have blessed me, so far, with four grandchildren. I see all of you in their eyes. They are strong spirited little ones who will grow to be as wonderful as you.

YOURSELF
Take care of yourself!
Make yourself happy; only you can do that.
You must love yourself in order to be loved.
Try not to worry over the little things and find laughter every day. "But most of all, I hope you dance".

MYSELF
I have accomplished so much in my life. I have not always had the easiest road to go down. I always asked God for guidance when I chose the next road. I have been so blessed and I am most thankful for all of you.

You are my pride and my joy. I love you all so much.

Mom

A THOUGHT FROM THE MOM'S CORNER
"You can fool some of the people some of the time, but you can't fool mom."   ***Author Unknown***

Betty Cottingham

Betty Cottingham
Bachelors of Science – Nursing – College of Mount St. Joseph (1956). Co-owner/Book keeper – family business. Mother of seven wonderful children and thirteen grandchildren. Director of Human Services for Campbell County, KY. Hobbies include gardening, cooking, bridge and traveling.

To my children,

At this stage of my life I look back and can see the hand of God guiding me. When life seemed most sorrowful or dangerous, positive elements emerged. I was ill with meningitis and pneumonia when seven years old, but being in Children's Hospital for six weeks gave me ambition to be a nurse and helped me to be a better mother.

I was the middle of seven children. I learned the art of compromise and appreciation of hard work. Your father and I opened a small business. This opportunity provided for us an avenue to serve the community, which we did in many ways.

The top values I encourage for you are:

FACE THE STORMS IN LIFE
Life is full of surprises, be prepared to face storms. Each of you has your own strengths and abilities. You have shown me that you are willing to work by being educated and following individual career paths. I am proud that each of you is an entrepreneur. You take risks and contribute to society in unique ways. You continue to amaze me with the lessons you teach me and help me to keep current. Be proud of your heritage.

To my Grandchildren,

One of my greatest joys of parenting is now being a Grandmother. It seemed marvelous to me the diverse personalities of my children; now I'm amazed by the variety of looks and personalities of thirteen "super children." Certainly genetics play a role, but I can see where love is the nurturing law. You show me love, respect, and hope for the future.

LOVE
Love each other and show kindness to all.

CHALLENGES
Be aware that life will give you many surprises, some good and others challenging. You show strength by how you meet the challenges.

SECRETS
Be wary of secrets; they can trap you. Better to be open and examine them.

DREAMS AND GOALS
Have dreams and set goals in life; small steps lead to giant rewards in time.

I pray each day for you.

Love,
Mom

Janeen Coyle

Janeen Coyle has been a fixture on Cincinnati Radio since "Columbus discovered the New World," she likes to joke! Actually about 34 years and she feels so fortunate to have spent all of those in her native Cincinnati, the world's greatest city! For the past 18 years Janeen has made it a family affair with her husband of 28 years, Chris, on WGRR's morning show "Married with Microphones." "The single most important thing I can do everyday is to make some one laugh in the morning," says Janeen. "With all the tragedy in the world, humor is a nice way to start the day." Janeen is involved in many charities including the Cincinnati SPCA to Ride Cincinnati for the Barrett Cancer Center at the University of Cincinnati, where she graduated a "few" years ago! Her favorite thing in life is being Mother to 25 year-old son Dylan and 5 year-old son Tank, the Pug. She also is 'Nana Jana" to step-son Chris's four beautiful children, Olivia, Will, Elizabeth and Andrew. Janeen is also the author of a new book on loving and losing a pet. The book available at Tate Publishing , bn.com and Amazon and is called "A Pug with a Plan," the true story of her Pugs, Frank and Tank.

To my Dearest Son, Dylan,

Know that: I can remember the day you were born like it was five minutes ago, holding you and feeling this overwhelming love. I kissed your day-old face and said, "I love you." I knew right then I would and will always go to the ends of the earth to protect you. Being your Mother has been the greatest joy of my life.

The top values I encourage for you are:

A GOOD HEART

How do you judge a person? I have one rule. Do they have a good heart? Are they kind and generous most of the time? We all fall short, but looking at the total landscape of a person's deeds will always help you forgive, if necessary. Be of good heart always.

FAITH

Whenever problems arise or whenever life is going your way, take time to praise and thank God. There is not a problem that you can't go to God with. Pray about anything and everything. Be yourself when you talk to God. There is no need for formalities. Pray and then turn it over to God, for tomorrow you will see things will get better. Don't worry about tomorrow today. Remember no one can steal your peace.

LOVE AND MARRIAGE

Love with all your heart. Be a good man, a good husband and a good involved father. Listen to your wife. Ask what you can do to help. Do the dishes, help with the laundry and vacuum the floor. This will go miles in making sure you have a good relationship. No one woman can do it all, not in today's world. Make decisions together and always be on the same page when it comes to parenting. Love is paramount, but even more important make sure your spouse will be an exemplary mother to your children. They deserve no less.

WORK

There is one tenet of work that has served me well. Never be a burden to the people and company you work for. Be a ray of sunshine to those that surround you on a daily basis. Don't complain or whine and if you do have a concern, take it to the person who can actually help. Work hard and be honest with the person that is buttering your bread. They deserve a good attitude and your best effort. Do what you love and love what you do and when those inevitable days of strife come, remember that's why they call it work. Stay away from whiners and don't worship the God of other people's opinion.

LOVING YOURSELF

I would encourage everyone to have a private love affair with themselves. This means treating yourself as well as you treat others. If you look good, say so. If you did something smart, say so, quietly of course. Pat yourself on the back. Treat yourself like you would treat a best friend. Give yourself a break, forgive mistakes and never beat yourself up. That's not what a best friend does. Be your own best friend.

Love, Mom

Cammy Dierking

Cammy Dierking - married to John for 25 years. Miami University: English and Journalism, 30 years as a TV broadcaster - one of the first women sportscasters in the country – the first in Nevada and Ohio. Evening News Anchor on WKRC-TV (CBS- Cincinnati), motivational speaker and emcee, co-author of "The Power of the Platform", avid cyclist, finished 15 marathons and 3 IRONMAN triathlons.

To my three beautiful, wonderful, and amazing daughters: Whitney, Casey, and Meg... ages 22,20, and 18,

Know that: Being your mom has been an incredible gift and has brought me such intense joy. You have taught me so much. Whit, you have a huge heart and are so kind and caring. You've shown me how to be more compassionate and less judgmental. Case, you are wise beyond your years, and it's often a challenge to keep up with you, intellectually! Also, your easygoing nature has forced me to be more patient and less controlling. And Meg, you are undoubtedly the sweetest person I know. I admire the way you have faced your fears and you've inspired me to do the same.

My love for each of you is strong and unconditional. No matter what happens, I will ALWAYS be here for you. You are the air in my lungs. My greatest hope is that I have given you two things: roots and wings.

I lost my mom to lung cancer when she was only 50. Two weeks later, I gave birth to my first daughter, Kylee. Three months later, Kylee died of SIDS. Those tragedies helped to reinforce just how important a mother is in her daughter's life, and vice versa. I have since been blessed with three more incredible daughters, and I NEVER take a single day with them for granted.

The top values I encourage for you are:
Health and fitness, confidence, a positive attitude, and sense of gratitude

GOOD HEALTH AND FITNESS
From the time you were born, Dad and I dragged you with us to the gym, the park, the pool, and dozens of races. OK, maybe it was partly because we didn't have a babysitter. But it was also to show you that fitness and living a healthy lifestyle should be a priority. It gives you energy and helps you feel good about yourself.

CONFIDENCE
Confidence can also empower and energize you. A lack of it can render you helpless. Each of you is worthy and deserving of happiness and success, and you are also resilient and able to cope with life's challenges. So believe in yourself the way I believe in you. Then go out and kick some butt!

A POSITIVE ATTITUDE AND SENSE OF GRATITUDE
I know you are tired of hearing me preach about this... but here it is again: Positive thoughts are so powerful. They lead to positive events, and positive outcomes. Conversely, negative thoughts become our demons and our roadblocks. And optimism, like gratitude, is really about paying attention to what's good, instead of what's not. You each have plenty of things to be grateful for... including the never-ending love and support of your old mom!

All my love,
Mom

Deborah Flynn

Deborah Flynn
Married to the love of her life – David for 40 years, mother of four daughters: Kate 35, Keely 33, and twins Rachel and Emily 26. She is "Grandmim" to 6 with one more on the way in December. Owner and founder of an online gift service, 4sistersgifts.com. Deb is happiest by the ocean surrounded by her family.

To Kate, Keely, Rachel, and Emily,

Know that: My proudest and greatest accomplishments are my children. When Dad and I first met it was love at first sight. We were blessed to be in the right place at the right time and I now realize how lucky we were to have found each other. I have always prayed you would find someone to go through life with who would love and respect you as much as we do each other.

The top values I encourage for you are:

FAMILY
Dad and I were married close to 5 years before we decided to have a baby. We knew when Kate came along that we were ready for this important responsibility. Our lives did change but so much for the better! Our focus now was Kate, a year and a half later Keely, and seven years later, the twins! As a parent you lose lots of sleep and personal time, but you gain so much more than you could ever imagine! The joy of watching that first smile, the first step, the first game, the performance, the graduations and all the significant passages of your lives have enriched ours more than we could have ever dreamed. The joke in our family, "Mom, who's your favorite?" is always funny but as you all become parents - if you do - you will see how your heart grows with each and every child.

SOCIAL MEDIA

Do you recall that you were the last of your friends to have an online account? The early days of online accounts were so enticing but Dad and I held out for a long time. Why? The answer is that we wanted to be the ones teaching you, influencing you and guiding you, not your friends. Times have changed. Email, Twitter, Facebook and the onslaught of social media have become such a force in our daily lives. My hope is that you put away the electronics often and speak to each other, listen to each other and always consider the source. If it is from someone you know, trust and respect, take it to heart. If not, ignore it. There is a lot of information floating about, much of it not helpful or accurate.

BEING YOURSELF

I am so proud of the four of you, all college grads and creating vibrant lives. Your kindnesses, consideration and thoughtfulness make being with you all a joy. It's okay to be smart; don't ever let anyone diminish your value by dismissing your ideas. You are fortunate to be living in a time where women are more valued than ever before. The partners you choose should be just that, partners in your journey. Take time for special things that give you pleasure. Life can be hard sometimes but the quiet moments, the normalcy of a safe haven, and people who will care and listen to you, these are the important things.

LIFE'S GOALS

Many of my friends have found contentment and success in their life's work; most have found that financial success alone does not bring fulfillment. The ones I know who live good, abundant lives are the ones that do not define themselves by what they do for a living but by how they live their lives. Be kind and helpful to others, as this will give you the most joy, as you grow older. There will always be people better off than you, and so many others less fortunate. Stop and consider what you can do to help. With love and gratitude that you are in my life, Mom xox

Keely Flynn

Keely is a Chicago playwright and blogger living in a fixer-upper that would make The Money Pit blush. Her site, Lollygag Blog, focuses on parenting, city living, and the daily hilarity of attempting to combine both. Her third cheerful bundle of sleep-deprivation arrives in December! She can also be found at Chicago Parent, Families In The Loop, The Little Style File, The SITS Girls, and napping in a blanket tent with her kids.

To Nora (age 4) & Susannah (age 2),

Know that: Baby girls, my life right now is ridiculously good. Staying home with you is a gargantuan part of that and inspires me every single day. (And totally beats the heck out of cocktail-slinging and faulty teleprompters, in case anyone asks.)

Although I don't always manage the "balance" thing, this job still wins. And even when one of you is standing on the kitchen table and another is Not Tired, in a pile of dumped-out puzzles, you need to know that there's nowhere else I'd rather be. Spending my days with you fills me with grateful joy - as do the choices I made to end up in this exact spot.

For an embarrassingly long time I strove for things that weren't making me happy. I invested in relationships that only made me lonelier, hammered away at goals that I thought I still wanted, and mirrored other people's "success" stories. Thankfully, I stopped that junk.

So, girls, here's my big ol' secret to you:

ATTAINING YOUR DREAM JOB

Although you should always fully commit to whatever you've chosen, certain things shouldn't feel like "work." Attaining your dream job is one of those things. You're creative, passionate little kids- I have no doubt that you'll embark on careers you'll love. And when you do, if you infuse your climb with enthusiasm, empathy, and global awareness, you'll find happiness almost every day. (Some days are just gonna be rotten, though. I am super sorry about that. On those days, just call your Mom.)

LOVE

Love is another one of those things that shouldn't feel like a burden. Yes, absolutely, being in a serious relationship demands attention, but it shouldn't ever drain you. Unless you're arguing about finances or who really should've taken out the recycling, relationships should feel like you've won the dating jackpot. And with whomever you chose to fight about the recycling, I have only one stipulation: they've got to realize how insanely wonderful you gals are, and want to work every day to help you be amazing. Really, that's it. Your Dad and I don't care what your future partners look, sound, or dance like, as long as they respect and make you wildly happy. And while I won't lie and say that money means nothing (because it can be rather nice), I met your Dad when we were both painfully broke actors and he always made me feel like we lacked for nothing. ("Wildly happy" can make things rather nice, too.)

IT BOILS DOWN TO THIS

I want you to be euphoric, as often as you can manage it. Surround yourself with happiness, imbue as much as possible into the world, and seek it out. If you can truly consider yourselves happy, you'll most likely have a nice handle on the big things: security, people who care for you, and an optimistic outlook.

And if the joy you strive for even approaches the elation that you've given our family, you'll be off to a fantastic start.

I love you,
Mom

Karen Rennegarbe Friedhoff

Karen Rennegarbe Friedhoff
- Married to Bob for 45 years
- Mother to Michael, David and Kenneth
- Mother-in-law to Heather and Melinda
- Grandmother to Sharon, Sean and Matthew
- Learning consultant and educator
- BS ED – University of Cincinnati
- Masters ED – Xavier University
- Life-long learner who loves life, storytelling, travel, family, friends and God.

To my family,

These are three values I hold precious in life:

FAITH

Believe in a Higher Power. God always gives His best to those who leave the choice with Him.

You all still chuckle at the simple, child's prayer Dad and I say at mealtime. It has been a constant in our home and I hope one in your home too.

Your faith will enhance your courage. Don't be afraid of life. Dare to believe that life is worth living and your faith will help you create that fact. Life is not the way it's supposed to be. It's the way it is. Faith, courage and the way you cope with life is what makes the difference. Courage doesn't always roar. Sometimes courage is the quiet voice of God encouraging you to try again tomorrow.

I remember sitting together with you in Church when you were small and the wonderful feeling of having you drape your arm on my shoulder, or holding hands and squeezing my hand with the 'secret signal,' or writing notes to each other during the service. I hope you will have some of those special moments with your children too.

My guiding principle: Proverbs 3: 5-6

Trust God from the bottom of your heart; don't try to figure out everything on your own. Listen for God's voice in everything you do, everywhere you go; He's the one who will keep you on track.

FAMILY

I am so proud of you and what you have accomplished! I feel that when you have your own children, you truly know how much I love you. You have a claim on my heart... as I'll always be your Mom.

Continue to share and remember the stories about our family: your father and me, grandparents and great-grandparents. Regardless of your relationship with family, you'll miss them when they're gone from your life....and give thanks for those brave immigrant ancestors that came to this country to make a better life!

Remember our yearly family vacations, our Friedhoff Family Olympics and the Official, Original, Fantastic, Friedhoff 'events' that we created. Remember the funny words we made up: 'whippy-doodle and putchy-potsch' made dessert-time fun! I still love to call and sing Happy Birthday to you on your birthday, wherever you are.

Enjoy children. Watch them closely, and you'll learn from them. If you focus on your family, the needs of others, your work and doing the very best you can, happiness will find you!

FRIENDS

No matter how serious your life requires you to be, everyone needs a friend to act goofy with!

I have great memories of the friends that have come into our home! Without friends you are missing out on a lot! Hold fast to the interlocking circle of those 'special' people. Don't be confused by friends and acquaintances; there is a difference!

You can always pray for a friend when you don't have the strength to help them in some other way.

Sincerely feel good about the success of others. Being able to feed good about the success of our friends allows us to accept it in our lives. It is our choice whether we are happy or not. Choose to be happy!

Kate Grant

Kate Grant
Married to Tom for 10 years and a stay-at-home mom to four fantastic boys.
Professional background in technology in education.
Volunteer and fundraiser for Williams College and serves on its Alumni Board.
Member of her sons' elementary school PTO and sits on their preschool's Board.

To my favorite kiddos in the whole world: Quinn (7), Cole (5), Declan (3) and Garrett (6 months),

Know that: Your dad and I were so thrilled to welcome each of you into this world. There's nothing better than your belly laughs, your smiles, and your hugs!

The top values I encourage for you are:

KEEP FAMILY FIRST
I hope you'll feel the abundant love your family has for you. There's nothing more important to me than family and I hope you'll grow up feeling the same. Family, both biological and the ones you choose, will experience life's joys and times of need alongside you. Family is your backbone, and a built-in support system to guide you every day. You're so lucky to be surrounded by folks who would do anything for you.

DO YOUR BEST
I hope you work hard, at school, in your career, playing sports, or enjoying volunteer work. If you give your best effort, I'll always be so proud, and I bet you will, too. Follow your passions and stay excited, because that will keep things fun.

STAY ACTIVE

I hope you remain active, healthy boys. Physical activity is something your Dad and I enjoy and we love to see you running around and having a blast, too. When on a team, be a team player and a good sport – nothing would make me prouder. Above all, I love to watch you play!

HELP OTHERS

I hope you're always as empathetic as you are today. It warms my heart how caring you are, both towards each other and to people in need. It's important to think about how we can help; I appreciate your excitement when gathering donations for the food bank, volunteering at school or sending care packages. We're so blessed in our lives so it's imperative that we give back however we can. This will help you keep a positive outlook; choosing happiness affects everyone around you! Everything else will fall into place if you start by looking for the good in others.

STAY CURIOUS

I hope that you are able to keep learning throughout life. You have natural curiosity that makes every experience interesting and keeps you wanting to know more. I treasure the small details in life that you notice and point out to me: a sliver of a rainbow reflected in our home, a dragonfly fluttering by, a carefully picked dandelion or wish flower, a single speck of glitter you discovered. Also, keep reading! It's a fabulous way to learn and to transport you to fun, far-off places.

KEEP A SONG IN YOUR HEART

I hope you'll always sing, dance and groove like you do today. Music is a big part of life for your Dad and me and we're thrilled to share that with you. Whether you play an instrument, sing in the shower or bust a move at family dance parties, keep rocking out!

I love you...you you you!
Love, Mom

Mary Greer

Mary Greer (nee Hall)
Birth Year: 1924
Education: Milliner
Career: Homemaker
Hobbies: music, reading, dancing, lively discussion.

To my daughter Suzanne,

Know that: You were born at a time of great strife, in England during the Second World War. Bombs fell steadily on the city of Reading where you were born. Your father was fighting on the front in Holland and Italy. Somehow my parents and I were able to obtain just enough extra rations to keep you healthy and well. As a war bride I traveled with you across the Atlantic with the war still raging in Europe. I arrived in the Northern Ontario town of Kirkland Lake. It was a rough and ready gold mining town with more taverns than churches, quite a shock for a well bred, sheltered young woman. We were welcomed and you thrived. You have grown and become my "B D" beautiful daughter both inside and out.

The top values I encourage for you are:

LOVE
Give unconditional love; treasure all of mankind's differences. See the uniqueness in every human being you encounter.

ART AND MUSIC
Let art and music become a part of you

Both have given me so much joy. The creativity that is in man is nothing less than a Miracle.

FORGIVENESS
Forgive yourself for the mistakes and missteps you make for it makes it so much easier to forgive others.

FRIENDS
Value your friendships for it is these friends who will sustain you and be there for you when life is both painful and pleasurable.

CHANGE
Don't fear the changes that life brings us because it is through change that we alter ourselves and learn to grow.

My wish for you is:
Good Health,
Strength to face adversity,
And Love.

"No life can be barren which hears the whisper of the wind in the branches, or the voice of the sea as it breaks upon the shore; and no soul can lack happiness looking up at the midnight stars." - William Winter

Love,
Mom

A THOUGHT FROM THE MOM'S CORNER
"My mother said to me, "If you are a soldier, you will become a general. If you are a monk, you will become the pope." Instead, I was a painter, and became Picasso"

Pablo Picasso

Brenda L. Hahn

Brenda L. Hahn

Married to Ben for 44 "awesome" years.
Graduated from Midway College.
Registered Nurse for 30 years.
Interests: Spending time with family and friends. UK Basketball fan - Go CATS!

To our three loving children, Troy, Tracy, and Trisha, their beloved spouses, Kristin, Mike, and Seth, and our beautiful grandchildren, Jared, Jordan, Taylor, Joel, Cooper, Jonah, Micah, Chloe, and Josie,

Know that:
I love you all so very much! I learned an acrostic, years ago, that I believe is worth sharing with each of you because it sums up and puts into perspective a very important life-long lesson. If you follow this advice it will lead you all into the arms of Jesus and to a place in Heaven to live eternally with God. Always remember "**JOY.**"

JOY
J – Put Jesus first in all that you do.
O – Put others second.
Y – Put yourself last.

Joy is the key to having fulfillment in your life and it will keep you on the pathway to life eternal.

I love each one of you, love spending time with you, and I can't imagine not having each one of you with me enjoying the blessings of Heaven, walking hand in hand with Jesus.

This is my greatest prayer for each of my dear loved ones.

Keep **JOU** in your life !!

All my love to each of you,
Mom / Nana

A THOUGHT FROM THE MOM'S CORNER

"The mother is everything - she is our consolation in sorrow, our hope in misery, and our strength in weakness. She is the source of love, mercy, sympathy, and forgiveness. He who loses his mother loses a pure soul who blesses and guards him constantly."

Kahlil Gibran

Denise Hall

Denise Hall
Born 1951 in Cincinnati, Ohio / Too many careers to list (short attention span) – currently a licensed Realtor with Comey & Shepherd / Volunteering includes boys' soccer coach, Terrace Park commissioner, Director: Cincinnati International Festival & no-kill animal shelter / Extended family: 2 dogs, their pet Ilene (a 3-legged cat) and Ilene's pets - gold fish & a frog / Enjoys old and new movies, reading, travel (usually to Montana), and most of all - time spent with family and friends!

To my son Ty Samuel,

Know that: I'm relishing this opportunity to impart my love for you, my pride in you as well as my heartfelt wishes for you.   Most importantly – know that I love you from the bottom of my heart – an infinite love.   My love for you is unwavering, absolute and always with you. Conceiving you was not easy - but you are my most cherished triumph.   Through you, I have truly learned life's immeasurable priorities - kindness, generosity, devotion, patience, hope and forgiveness. It is my hope that these values play an ever-increasing part in your life.

The top values I encourage for you are:

FAMILY AND FRIENDS
Someone said, "You don't get to pick your family." True – but if you could, I hope you would pick us again. Your family is your steadfast foundation – your refuge when life's path is painful and unsure. Family is always here for you.   You do, however, get to choose your friends. Value your bona fide friends and as years go by – make the effort to keep in touch with them. Be there for each other and try to not burn bridges.   Loving family and genuine friends are a rare treasure and always worth fostering.

LIFE
Life flies by............so try to enjoy and achieve something each and every day. (Easier said than done.) I hope you find a balance between taking important things seriously and letting go of the worrisome stuff – much of which you can't change anyway. I hope you find work that you enjoy – work hard and learn the value of satisfaction. Play.......no matter what your age. Play with your spouse, your children, your friends! Keep those ice skates, hockey stick and puck near-by.... It's your most "natural" sport – please don't stop playing. One of my greatest joys has been watching you play hundreds of hockey games............it has always been fantastic!

YOU ARE BLESSED
Ty, you are blessed. You're physically sound and strong, bright and inventive, handsome and adventurous. You are easy to be with, calm, humorous, caring and generous. Use these God-given qualities to enhance the richness of your life. Share these attributes with your family and friends – incorporate these strengths in your work. These special ingredients will help assure a successful recipe for life.

My ultimate hope in my life evolves around you. I hope that to some small degree I've shown you the value of parental love. I hope I've eased your pain when disappointments have knocked at your door. I hope that occasionally I've given you sage advice and a basic understanding of what really matters in your life. Last but not least – I hope I've given you unparalleled love. You've done all these things for me.

Love,
Mom

Diane Hample

Diane Hample

Colerain High School and BFA: Edgecliff College.
Volunteer parent mentor for families who have children with Downs Syndrome / Downs Syndrome Association.
Hobbies: ballroom dancing and gardening.

To my precious children: Nick, Lauren, and Colleen,

Know that: each of you is a unique and special gift from God. The most important thing that I hope you will always remember is to trust in God. Put your faith in God and know that things will turn out right.

The top values I encourage for you are:

TRUST GOD
When things get hard in life, and when you don't receive what you are praying for, know that maybe in your best interests, it is better not to have your prayer answered. God's plan is not always the same as ours, but His plan for your life is always right. Trust in God; have faith in God, always.

BLESSINGS IN DISGUISE
Thank you for so many happy, wonderful times together. Each of you has brought me so much joy and pride over the years. The source of pride has changed as you have grown from children into adults, but the feeling is always the same. I admire the kindness and compassion you show to others and the sensitive hearts you all have, especially evidenced in how you relate to your sister, Colleen. Watching you read to her or talk to her warms my heart. Colleen is a special, beautiful child. It is a true joy and blessing to know her. She brightens up the room

with her sweet smile. I have learned that sometimes God gives us blessings in disguise.

When I think back to when Colleen was born and how afraid I was about her future, I wish I could have known then how wonderful she would be. Although there have been challenges to face, it has been the challenges that have made the successes all the more rewarding. Having you, Colleen, has taught me to appreciate the beauty in simple things. Thank you for your smile, your laugh, your hand to hold, your sweet face to kiss goodnight. I love you so much.

KINDNESS
Thank you, Nick, for being such a wonderful big brother. You are a kind and sensitive young man. I am so proud of who you are today. I love you.

SHARE YOUR TALENTS
Thank you, Lauren, for sharing your talent and joy with all of us. You are an amazingly gifted artist and an inspiring, young woman. You have brought us all so much happiness. I love you.

BE THANKFUL
Nick, Lauren, and Colleen, thank you all for making my life so rewarding and for giving me so much to be thankful for.

Love,
Mom

Gerri Harbison

Gerri, her husband Mike and family have been Montgomery Ohio residents since 1985. Gerri is a licensed Realtor with Huff Realty and a Hospice of Cincinnati volunteer. She was a member of the Bicentennial Commission in 1994-95 and has chaired the Montgomery 4th of July Festival in the Park since 1995, the Bastille Day Celebration in 1999 and the Sister Cities Commission from 1997-99 after joining Sister Cities in 1996. She was elected to City Council in 1999, served as Mayor of Montgomery from December 5, 2005, through December 7, 2011 and remains a City Council Member.

To my children, Steve, Mike, Walt, Brian, and Jessica, ages 30 to 52 and my eight grandchildren: even though we are a very blended family, I love all five of "our" kids in very different ways. You are all very special to me, each in your own way, and you mean so much to me whether I gave birth to you or not.

Know that: To "our" boys, while I would never step on your Mom's toes, I hope that I have had some influence in your lives throughout the last 33 years because you certainly have had an influence in my life throughout that time. And to my girl, Jessica, you have been the light of my life since I first felt you move inside me. I am the person I am today because you have believed in me. And to all of you, I know that you all have different struggles that you go through on a daily basis, but I also know you are very smart and up to those challenges and struggles. Those of you who have had children have raised beautiful families and have put your own unique personality into raising wonderful children.

The top values I encourage for you are:

BEING TRUE
Always be true to yourself. There are no perfect parents in this world; we can only do the best we can. We have

some successes and we have some things that are not so successful. If you make a decision, whether it is popular or unpopular in your life, as long as you can look yourself in the eye in the mirror without hesitation and know you have done the right thing for you, then you have made the right decision in your life.

DISAPPOINTMENTS
So often in daily life, we have disappointments or rough patches but instead of looking at them as failures, if we can look at each experience as a learning tool, and ask ourselves, "What am I supposed to learn from this experience, whether it is good or bad?" --then that can help guide you through the good times and the bad times.

MARRIAGE
You are all so very smart and talented in your own lives. So very successful! I know that marriage has been a hard thing in some of your lives and it is not as easy as it looks at times. Your dad and I have been married for 32 years, and it can be hard every day to make things work, but when you do work at it, then it will be another piece of your life of which to be proud. It is easy to throw in the towel, but hang in there with the faith that you have, that you are in the place you are supposed to be, and that God has you there for a very specific reason. That is what is important. You can work through the differences, and you will come out on the other side better for the time and commitment you have put into such an important relationship.

I will leave you with a few of the lyrics from a song that I really like, called "If I Could" by Ray Charles:

> If I could, I would teach you all the things I never learned,
> And I'd help you cross the bridges that I burned.
> If I could, Yes, I would.

All my love,
Mom/Gerri

Paula Hawley

Paula Hawley, maiden name Enghauser
Born 1966
1984 - HS, Academy of the Holy Names
1988 - BA, German, Baylor University
1989 – Air Force, Specialty School,
Goodfellow AFB
CAREER - Air Force Active Duty Officer–
1989 – 1995; stay at home Mom when
you were little; Air National Guard/Air
Force Reservist - 2000 to present. Since
2003- Analyst with a US Federal
Agency;
HOBBIES – Travel, Walking/Hiking
Outdoors, Jogging, Decorating, Cooking,
Reading

To my daughters Molly (17 years of age), and Emma (13 years of age),

Know that: Having you both as my daughters has been the highlight of my life, and being your mom has been what matters most. With life's ups and downs, you have prevailed and grown into such beautiful young women. I am so proud of you, and I thank God for choosing me to be your mom. There are some days, with hindsight, that I was not the best example for you—for that I am sorry, but understand that it has been a deep hunger within me to "know better" so that I can "do better" in this life, and more importantly, for you. I have prayed often for you and I know the commands of God are instilled in your hearts; He will direct your path if you let Him. The love I have for you is constant; it is one of those forever things in an ever-changing world, and nothing you "do" or "don't do", "say" or "don't say", will affect this. I love you the same no matter what.

The top values I encourage for you are:

KEEP BALANCE IN YOUR LIFE
Life can be so overwhelming, and as women, young and old, we often forget to take care of ourselves as we scramble to balance our priorities and commitments to work, family, friends, and community. Lean on your friends and family when times are tough. Take some time each day just for you, when stressful times arrive, and they will. —A bubble bath with a good book is

much better for you than reality TV and a bag of chips! Exercise your mind and body regularly; it will keep your brain sharp, and your body strong. But most importantly feed your soul; be still and seek a connection with God through prayer or mediation daily—He is (and always will be) what carries you through this life.

BEAUTY LIES WITHIN

Beauty is not dependent on what we wear or whether we are having a good hair day. Our beauty as human beings, as women, lies within. As you continue to grow, and become more accepting and aware of yourself, that is, your strengths *and* your weaknesses, you will then understand others better, and be more accepting of them. Your efforts in personal growth, feed this "beauty" within, and it becomes evident when you can be kind when someone is unkind, when you forgive something that seemed unforgivable, and when you take your eyes off of yourself and show compassion and love to those that are hurting. When we are young, we forget that our physical beauty will fade—so nurture that beauty within and know it has the potential to blossom and grow beyond our understanding.

IT'S YOUR LIFE, YOU GET TO CHOOSE, BE PROACTIVE, AND CONCENTRATE ON WHAT YOU CAN CHANGE

Be proactive in your life. Although it is natural to avoid things that are unpleasant and difficult, it is much more rewarding and less anxiety-provoking to be proactive in your daily living. I know that practicing this will bring you more contentment and success. The good news is that you have control over what you choose to do each day, each step of the way—you choose how to react to what life throws your way; you choose the response--the thoughts, and the emotions. Ask yourself, did I learn something here? Or is there something I can do differently next time I am in this situation? Or you can go the other direction, and choose to be angry, hurt, and bitter. We cannot control other people, nor can we change them. However, by being your best, and learning along the way, you no doubt will affect people in a positive way. Instead of worrying about other people's actions, and trying to predict or control their behavior, it is far more effective to concentrate on what we can change—ourselves. Spend your energies on your response, on your inner thoughts, and behaviors, and never blame others for the circumstances in your life.

I love you both more than you can ever imagine, Mom

Rita Heikenfeld

Rita Nader Heikenfeld, CCP, CMH, is an award winning syndicated journalist, accredited family herbalist, author, cooking teacher, media personality and the founding editor of www.Abouteating.com. Rita writes a syndicated weekly column for Community Press Newspapers. Rita is Resident Herbalist for Fox 19 Morning Xtra, Natorp's, Earthineer and Granny's Garden, and is listed in Who's Who in the Midwest. Rita is a former adjunct professor at The University of Cincinnati and can be found on Sacred Heart Radio.

She lives "in the sticks" outside of Batavia, Ohio, with her family, where they heat with wood, raise chickens for eggs, and grow their own produce and herbs. Rita considers her most important achievement being a wife, mother and grandmom!

To my sons Joe, Jason and Shane,

Know that: When I think of what is non-negotiable in my life, family comes to mind. You have brought more joy, pride and love into Dad's and my life than you would ever imagine. When you were young, we could see the potential of what you could become, and you have not disappointed. You are wonderful fathers and loving husbands. We could not have hand picked better wives: Inge for Joe, Jessie for Jason and Courtney for Shane. Loving mothers, all. And the grandchildren you have blessed us with are among our most precious gifts.

Here is what my heart wishes for you and yours:

NEVER STOP DREAMING! FANTASIZE! IMAGINE!
Remember the "Jack and the Beanstalk" beans we planted when you were children? We tied strings to the second story bedroom window and anchored them in the ground next to the seeds so that the seeds could climb up to the window and beyond, perhaps up to heaven! Share that sense of fantasy with your children. Know that you are never too "grown up" to have dreams. Dreams do not have deadlines. Dreams become goals, and dreamers become creators.

NURTURE NATURE
I love that you embrace and respect the beauty and wonder of nature with your children. This gives them a sense of spirituality

and lets them know the value of being good stewards of their environment. Identifying (and yes, tasting) wild edibles, turning the earth with a spade, picking a flower and seeing the symmetry in each petal, or netting crayfish in the river keeps us in tune with nature's song.

BE COURAGEOUS
Teaching children to be confident is easier, I think, than teaching them courage. Be courageous in your own endeavors. That's the best example of all. Encourage your children to go beyond their comfort zone to achieve a goal. The exploration of the process itself will give them confidence. "Shoot for the moon, and even if you don't succeed, you'll still land among the stars!"

CHERISH THE ORDINARY
It's not the special occasions that keep us close and create memories, but the ordinary, everyday happenings: Sunday dinners, reading books together, biking through the neighborhood, helping with homework.

CELEBRATE FAMILY HISTORY
We are descended from adventurous and brave immigrants. Let the children help with meals and tell them the meaning of a special dish, like the Lebanese green beans we serve as baby's first table food, or why Dad calls his German version of French toast "Blindfish."

PRAY
Without prayer, life would be empty indeed. Pray together. Prayer can take many forms, from the memorized prayers to the "help me" or "thank you" prayers. Pray for guidance *and* faith daily. The wisdom of my years tells me that even the most challenging days have sparks of good in them. Remember that as you pray nightly prayers. Most of all, know that the love I have for you is the purest love of all: A mother's love.

Love, Mom

Jean Hellyer

(Jean) Regina Hellyer (nee Enghauser). BA: Xavier University (Edgecliff). MEd: University of Cincinnati. CAREER PATH- Assistant Professor of English University of Cincinnati and Co-director Reading and Study Skills Labs; Co-author of national Study Skills textbooks; Adjunct Professor, Chatfield College and Northern KY University. HOBBIES – writing, dancing, reading, gardening, visiting grandchildren.

*T*o my extraordinary daughters Melissa, Susan, Karen, and my amazing sons-in-law Jeff, Darren, and Paul. With a special dedication to my most precious grandchildren Kayla, Nicholas, Nathan, Marisa, Connor, Tyler, Ivan, and Meeka,

Know that: My life would not be complete without all of you in it. You, my daughters, have grown into beautiful, loving, capable women, and have chosen good, outstanding men as husbands. I am so proud of all of you and the talents and moral values you bring to this world.

The top values I encourage for you are:
FAMILY
Cherish your family above all: Eat together. Celebrate special moments. Create unique family traditions. Talk to each other with love, interest, and concern. Give warm greetings and farewells each day. Laugh and cry together; work and play together. Pray together.
GOOD CHARACTER
Always remember who you are and be proud of who you are. "You were born to become the-best-version-of-yourself" (Matthew Kelly). Circumstances, time, and other people can test your good character, but strive to maintain your integrity throughout these challenges. "Character is what you do when no one is watching."
HONESTY
Always give and expect the truth in all of your relationships. This is vital especially with your spouse,

children, and siblings. Otherwise, small lies become big lies and soon the foundation of love can be weakened or broken. Trust and love are built on truth. Secrets, by their very nature, destroy relationships.

GRATITUDE

Openly, regularly, express your appreciation. Say "Thank you" to others-- for the steady loving care from your spouse, for the contributions from your children, for those who serve or fulfill you in other ways. Express your gratitude to God everyday for His gift of these wonderful people in your life.

LIFELONG LEARNING

All learning—formal and informal-- can open doors and make the seemingly impossible, possible. Read, take courses, research, write, train, observe, travel, ask for help, seek counseling…. "The more we know, the more we realize how much we don't know."

WORK AND MONEY

No matter how demanding, important, or fulfilling your career is, always put your family first: they are your life-long investment. At the end of the day, intrinsic rewards will make you rich. Work hard and do your very best, whether or not you collect a paycheck.

Live within your means and don't let marketing tricks override your common sense. Shop wisely and make long-term savings a habit. When possible, give back through financial support and by volunteering your time and talents.

CREATIVITY

Let music, dance, writing, art, cooking, gardening, crafts, or other creative outlets inspire you. It doesn't matter how good you are at these; it only matters that you wrap yourself in the bliss of creativity. "Dance like no one is watching, sing like no one is listening, and love like you've never been hurt."

With all my love and admiration for you,
Mom, Jean, Grandma/Grammy

Julie House

Julie House is the Founder of Equipped Ministries, a health and wellness ministry founded on the principles of 2 Timothy 3:16, 17. "The Bible is a useful tool for teaching," and "we are thoroughly equipped for every good work." (And that includes losing weight and living healthy!) She writes weekly as a guest columnist for the Community Press and has a passion for Christ and family. After her brother's untimely death in 2009, it has also become her life's mission to share her story of experiencing miracles in the midst of tragedy, family, alcoholism and homelessness. Julie has a passion for sharing her testimonies and speaks often for Women's Seminars, churches and community events.

*T*o my true gifts from God: Grace, Jonah and Emmiefaith,

What a blessing and honor to be able to write to you in this way. I often think of the values, skills, beliefs, morals and lessons I long to pass onto you as a mother. Although it's nearly impossible to narrow down my hopes and dreams for you, may the following be a light for your path and a map for your road. May you know the love I have for you goes beyond what words can describe, and my heart bubbles over at the gift of living this life as your mom! I love you forever!

My prayers, hopes and dreams for each of you:

THE GREATEST BOOK ON EARTH
There is nothing I want to leave more deeply embedded in your soul than the breathtaking words of the Bible. There are no greater lessons I could teach you, no better nourishment for your soul. My own greatest lessons and hopes have been pulled from God's inspired word. If you carry one prized possession with you wherever you go, may it be your Bible.

GOD CAN BE TRUSTED

Hold tightly to God is this life. His word is filled with promises just for you and just as He says, "He can be trusted to keep His promises." [Hebrews 10:23]

YOUR FUTURE IS SO BRIGHT

Always strive to be more, do more, and live life more fully. When you doubt your future, your path in life, hold firmly to Jeremiah 29:11 and always remember God's plans for you have always been and continue to be about great hope, success and a wonderful future.

GOD'S GOT THIS

Problems will arise in this lifetime. Temptations will cross your paths all too often. As you encounter life's difficulties and possibly even tragedies, hold firmly to John 16:33, "In this life you will have trials and sorrows, but take heart, I have overcome the world." When the temptations seem too strong always know that God's word promises, "He will not allow the temptation to be more than you can stand." *And,* he will "show you a way out so that you can endure." [1 Corinthians 10:13]

ABOVE ALL: LOVE

It won't always be easy to love, fun to love, and you may not always want to love. But the greatest gift I can pass onto you is the lesson that we learn through the crucifixion of our Savior, and a lesson that was reiterated for me at the loss of your Uncle Jimmy. There are no conditions to love. We love others **SIMPLY** because Christ loves us!

Love, Mom

Mary Jean Howard

(Mary) Jean Howard (nee Enghauser) was born in 1944 in Cincinnati, Ohio, and raised in Westwood. In 1977 she immigrated to Toronto, Canada, where she married the love of her life, Paul Howard, an Ottawa native, who had lived several years in the States, in Washington, D.C., New Orleans, and St. Louis. They have been very happily married for 35 years and are blessed in every way with these 3 wonderful daughters and 4 grandchildren. Both Paul and Mary spent happy careers in high school education and continue teaching adults in their Catholic parish community. Traveling, gardening, decorating, reading, and writing rank among her top interests.

*T*o my three daughters, Andrea, Colleen and Bernadette, at the ages of 33, 31 and 28, all living near the Toronto area,

Know that: I am writing this on October 4, 2012, on the 71st wedding anniversary of your grandparents, George and Bertha Enghauser. May they rest in peace, knowing that their good lives were passed on in perpetuity; and in this 35th year of the marriage of your parents, Jean and Paul Howard. Each of your births was a rebirth for your Dad and me. That we could create new life in the unique person that each of you are, was nothing short of a miracle and a total gift from God. We have rejoiced at each step along your journey! At your present ages of 28, 31, and 33, you are in the bloom of your own life and we wish you God-speed on the road ahead of you.

If we had a legacy or advice to leave with you, whether overtly or subtly, it would certainly include the following –

PUT FAMILY FIRST
Love yourself and you will be able to love your spouse and your children, and other persons you meet.

REALIZE THAT YOU CANNOT HAVE IT ALL
But you have it in your power for all to have.

HAVE AN ATTITUDE OF GRATITUDE FOR ALL YOU HAVE RECEIVED

Know that you are abundantly blessed by God, so pass it on.

KEEP FOCUSED ON THAT WHICH LASTS, THAT WHICH ENDURES

When all else may be taken from you.

ON A PRACTICAL LEVEL

Dine together at family meals, listen carefully to each other's story.

Don't just tolerate each other, but cherish one other.

Celebrate special days and special milestones.

Praise, compliment, support, but challenge each other to grow.

"Be the change you wish to see in the world." (Gandhi)

Step up to the plate, do your part, and then offer even more.

Take care of yourself -- you'll then be able to care for others.

Never go to bed angry-- reconcile your differences.

Hug each other often, kiss your partner good-night.

Never quit or resign under pressure.

Follow your conscience, but have a conversation with God first and often.

Expand your mind, expand your heart, expand your perspective.

Grow with your partner.

Live what you want your children to learn.

Hold your kids responsible and forgive their shortcomings.

Send them forth with an apple and a road map.

Always welcome them home to your heart.

LIVE, LOVE, LAUGH, LEARN, LEAVE YOUR OWN LEGACY!

With All my Love, Mom

Julie Hubbard

-Married to Rick Hubbard for 26 happy years!
-Educator for 26 years and counting (20 years classroom teacher, 1 year instructional coach, 4 years principal, 1 year
-Director of Curriculum and Assessment)
-Blessed by every child I've had the privilege to teach.
-Member of Christ Baptist Church

To my 24-year-old daughter, Shea, and my 20-year-old son, Tyler.

Know that: Your dad and I were both raised by Christian parents who created a loving home rooted in faith in God. We have tried to create this same atmosphere for both of you. From the moment you were born we realized the magnitude of our responsibility to provide you with unconditional love for the rest of your lives. You have both made that an easy task. I pray for you daily and desire that you both follow Christ's will for your lives.

CAREER
It is a true blessing to have a career that you are passionate about and love. I have always hoped that each of you would choose a career that you loved and brought you happiness. Shea, as a teacher, I know that you have chosen the right career because I hear it in your voice when you talk about the students you serve. You are a natural and so many children are going to be lucky to have you as their teacher. Tyler, I can't imagine you doing anything else but flying. The first time you flew at EKU and called me to tell me all about it I knew by the enthusiasm and excitement in your voice you had made the right career choice. Being a pilot is the perfect fit for you. My heart is full knowing you have both followed your passions.

FAMILY
Remember your roots, remember the importance of family connections, and remember we love having you

both home for special events or just to hang out. Our time together is precious and appreciated.

DO UNTO OTHERS

I remember taking strawberries to a friend and Tyler asked me if she was old or sick. I asked why and he said that is who you always help out. We need to all remember the importance of helping those in need and treating everyone with respect and love.

COUNT YOUR BLESSINGS

I always tried to teach you to stop and enjoy the beauty of a sunset and to never take its beauty for granted. I hope you treat life in that same manner. Time goes fast so you must make it a priority to stop, appreciate, and enjoy the beauty around you. Count your blessings, name them one by one, count your many blessings, see what God has done.

Shea,

Since you were very young you have always been so independent. You somehow taught yourself to read at age 4 and I knew then you were going to figure things out with or without me. You are still so brave and independent. I am impressed by your willingness to travel and experience new cultures and people. You are smart, beautiful and full of life. You make me proud.

Tyler,

Since you were very young you have been a very determined individual. To be honest, that characteristic made you a somewhat difficult toddler. I remember saying through tears one night that your determination would serve you well as an adult, but as a toddler it was about to get the best of me. I was so right. Your determination is serving you very well as an adult. You are focused and you know what you want and how to work to get it. You make me proud.

FAVORITE BIBLE VERSE FOR YOU

For by grace you have been saved through faith. And this is not your own doing; it is the gift of God, not a result of work, so that no one may boast. Ephesians 2:8-9

All my love, Mom

Jenn Jordan

Jenn Jordan
Co-Host of the Jeff and Jenn Morning Show on Cincinnati's Q102 since 2002.
Graduate of Eastern Illinois University and a 25-year radio veteran who spends much of her free time advocating for those living with Autism.

Jakob is 11 years old and was diagnosed 8 years ago with moderate-severe Autism and Apraxia. He started speaking when he was 6 and is able to answer who, what, where and when questions but has yet to answer how and why. His speech can be difficult to understand but he and I have developed our own language it seems. It's something we work on every day. I do a home-based program with him called Son Rise and he's involved in multiple therapies. He's come a long way from where we started and I couldn't be more proud.

To my son, Jakob,

Dude,
I have never in my whole life been with someone who could make me laugh harder, smile wider or know true love more than you. You are my light, my inspiration and my best friend.
I'm pretty sure that in this relationship, you're the teacher and I'm the student who has so very much to learn. While I have been on this planet longer than you and I may know how to play the game, you are the one with the spirit, the fire and the knowing of what life is really about...the seeking of and experiencing joy in each moment. That appears to be your quest at every turn and I've never met anyone who's clearer about what makes them happy. And I love that once you know, there isn't a soul who can stop you from going after it. You're brave, confident and unyielding.

You're my little non-conformist who inspires me to not care quite so much about what other people think. I know you'll eventually get me there. You give me the courage to let my freak flag fly. Yeah, I'm quirky, I'm weird and so what? Life is short and I'm gonna do the things I love regardless of differences between a little kiss, a big kiss and a huge kiss. I love your smile, your belly laugh and when you look me in the eye and see right through me. I love it when we walk into Kroger and the first thing you do is look to see what the neighbors think. You do that every day and you do it big. It's awesome.

I love it when you show me the checkout lanes are open and then take forever to decide which one you wanna go through.

I love that you're mine. I think you're perfect, wonderful and amazing. There isn't a thing I would change about our journey together through this adventure called autism. How lucky we are to have been blessed to do this together...slow and simple, with joy and laughter leading the way. It may not always be easy but nothing worth having is. And you, my beautiful child, are so worth everything I have and everything I am. Thank you for just being you and standing firm in the knowing that you are enough, just as you are. In fact, you are far more than enough. You are the greatest gift I have ever been given.

With all my Love, Mom

Alice Ketterer

Alice Ketterer (nee Wagonlander)
Born 1927
Married to Charlie for 51 years
Housewife –
Actmedia/ Shillitos/
Klosterman's Bake Shops – Mgr /
Delta
Interests: Singing / home / repairs /
cooking/sketching/sewing

*T*o my five wonderful kids: Chuck, Maria, Tom, Debbie and Paul (between the ages of 59 and 67),

Know that: What you all have done for me is unbelievable. Here I am 87 years old and I have caused you a lot of problems with my health and now falling on top of that. But you have stuck with me through it all. I really, really love every single one of you with all my heart and soul.

The top values I encourage for you are:

GOD
I have all the faith in the world in God.
If you believe in God and put your trust in Him, you will get through just fine.

GOOD WORK ETHIC
One way that you can get ahead is to stick together and work together. Charlie was a very hard-working man, and I think that I was a hard worker too. I painted roofs and tore garages down and put siding on the house and fixed cement in the front. I think that is one way you can get ahead -- through hard work.

FAMILY
I have made so many, many mistakes through my life, but you kids have forgiven me for them. You have stuck by me and I love each and every one of you. I have tried hard. We have had some great family meals and get-togethers at my house, even after Charlie passed. Now it is up to you kids to have the family to each of your own homes.
The most important thing is love, and trust, forgiveness, hanging in there with each other, and helping each other whenever you need help. When the job is too big and you know you need help, then it is time that you all put your efforts together and do the job together.

EDUCATION
I'd encourage anyone to get the best education you can. I wish I would have gone after a higher education, but back in my days it wasn't stressed as much. And we all had to go to work earlier in life just to keep food on the table. A good education will give you many more opportunities in life and it is something no one else can ever take away from you.

I would work my fingers to the bone for any of my children, which I love more than life itself.

All my love,
Mom

A THOUGHT FROM THE MOM'S CORNER
"My mother was the most beautiful woman I ever saw. All I am I owe to my mother. I attribute all my success in life to the moral, intellectual and physical education I received from her." *George Washington*

Jackie Cummings Koski

Jackie Cummings Koski
Born: Aiken, South Carolina
Degree: BA from Augusta State University
Account Executive –LexisNexis, Dayton, Ohio
Author of award-winning book,
"Money Letters 2 my Daughter"
Speaker/Financial Literacy Advocate
One Daughter: Amber Koski, Age 17

Hobbies/Talents: Writing, Investing/Stocks,
Financial Education, Creative Media, Traveling

Dear Amber,

Know that: For me, the journey of motherhood hasn't been easy, but it's been filled with so many memorable moments that have shaped who we both are today. Since that hot day in July, over 17 years ago when I first heard you cry, I always asked myself this question: "Am I a good mom?" I've learned that I don't have the answer; only you do. With that in mind, all I ever wanted to do was teach you the values and lessons I believe will help you achieve the greatest success in life—all with love and from the heart. Let me remind you of just a few.

The top values I encourage for you are:

NO MATTER HOW MUCH OR LITTLE YOU MAKE, ALWAYS SAVE SOMETHING

I started teaching you this when you were little and made you save half of your allowance and spend and enjoy the other half. By the time you were 16, you had enough money saved to help pay for your first car. I saw in your face how proud you were to have some of your own money going towards the purchase of your newly found "freedom on four wheels."

STAND UP FOR WHAT YOU BELIEVE IS RIGHT

When you were a junior in high school a substitute teacher accused you of something you insisted never happened and you were suspended from school for five days for it. You were so adamant about your innocence, so I wanted you to know that you should fight for what you believe. We took your dispute to the highest authority we knew to be available to us, and that was the school district superintendent. I made sure you knew the outcome might not be in your favor, but you can never back down just because there's a chance you might lose. Well, we pleaded our case but the superintendent did not give us a break. One point for the school, and no points for the Mother-Daughter Koski team...can't win 'em all.

YOU MUST INSIST ON BEING TREATED FAIR: IT'S ALWAYS NOT A GIVEN

This was tested your senior year in high school with your cheerleading tryouts. You had been cheering your entire high school career, but were strangely cut from the senior cheer squad...hmmm? This set off a chain of events filled with a temperament of "heck no, not my daughter!", and the teachable moments began. I started by sitting you down and getting your side of the story (facts only requested). This was hard because you were clearly crushed and holding back the tears. I then went on a fact-finding mission ONLY (not to accuse anyone of anything) with the athletic director to get the school's side of the story. After unraveling everything, the school board found it necessary to move to a more objective process, effective immediately. That meant...you were back on the squad. There was no way THIS mom was going to let anyone treat my daughter anything less than fair! "Heck no, not my daughter!"

I don't know if you will think the way I raised you was good, bad or indifferent; but it was done with love. As a mother, I have questioned myself a hundred times, and often fought between thinking I was being too hard and too easy on you at the same time. What a journey so far and I am anxious to for the next chapter.

Love,
Mom - still wondering if she did a good job

Jackie Lang

Born in 1960 in Cincinnati, Ohio.
Married 25 years to husband, James
BSN and MSN, University of Cincinnati
CAREER: Practice Manager Greater Cincinnati Internal Medicine, Inc., Clinical-Nurse Specialist, Nursing Instructor.
COMMUNITY: Serving as a Montgomery Woman's Club Officer, Served as PTO President twice, Served on City of Montgomery Parks & Recreation Commission.
HOBBIES: Spending time with family and friends, reading, volunteering in the community.

To my beloved children: Rachel, Victoria, Rebecca, Stephanie, and Michael,

Know that: You are the "sunshine of my life" and each one of you knows how much I truly love you. You have given me more joy than I ever thought possible. Each of you has opened my world to the world of possibilities. Each of you has been a teacher and a role model to me. It has been through your eyes, your perspectives, and your wisdom, that I am a better listener and more open to the world around me.

LEARNING

Life is all about learning and discovery. It is about learning who you are and who you want to become in life. Your education doesn't just come from the classroom or the textbooks. Your education includes all of your life experiences, your triumphs and your failures. Every experience helps to shape you into the person you are becoming. What you take away from those experiences and how you handle them will help to determine your responses to situations in the future. The Greek philosopher, Epictetus once stated, "It is not what happens to you but how you react to it that matters." Life is hard and often seems to be unfair. No one is exempt. Disappointments and bad stuff are always going to happen. Don't get hung up on the temporary failures and don't overvalue your successes. You are so much more than either of them. Use them both to shape yourself into the person you want to become. They will help you to become proactive rather than reactive in dealing with new situations.

RESOURCES

It is okay to ask for help. Don't be afraid to seek out resources. Contrary to what you might have heard, smart people don't know everything. Smart people are smart because they know where to find the resources they need, are not afraid to tap those resources, and are secure enough to give credit where credit is due.

SMART CHOICES

By making SMART CHOICES, you will become the best person you can be. Remember:

Spirituality: Believe in your faith and trust in God. Prayer can sustain you through very difficult times.

Money: Know the value of money, spending wisely, and saving for the future.

Action: Don't be afraid to take action. Nothing gets accomplished by sitting on the fence.

Respect: Show respect to others, their beliefs, and their traditions. Respect your country and those who serve it. Always respect yourself and your body.

Thankful: Treasure the moments and be thankful for your blessings.

Character: Be a person of character and integrity. Be honest and be truthful.

Humble: Be humble of your achievements and give credit where credit is due.

Optimism: Have a positive attitude.

Inclusive: Be inclusive and not exclusive in your interactions with others.

Compassion: Show compassion and always be willing to help others.

Education: Take every opportunity to educate yourself and be willing to give of your time and talents to help educate others.

Surround: Surround yourself with good people and good role models.

Remember, your family is one of the greatest gifts you have been given. Always cherish your family and always include them in your life.

Finally, my wish for you is that each of you finds the love of a good person. I am so truly blessed to have the love of my life, your father. Relationships require work and compromise. There are good days and difficult days, but the love and companionship of a good person is definitely worth the effort.

Rachel, Victoria, Rebecca, Stephanie, and Michael, I love you with my whole heart. I am so very proud of each and every one of you. You are indeed, as your father always says, "Our greatest treasure"!

Love, Mom

Marilyn Marie Leal

Marilyn Marie Leal
Born in 1961 in Cincinnati.
Mother of 3
Cardiology nurse at The Christ Hospital
Heart & Vascular
Independent Legal Nurse Consultant
Shaklee Distributor

To the joys of my heart:
Nathan, Meredith, Cathryn, and now my dear
granddaughters, Everleigh and Kenzley,

Know that: We have a little song that is special to us that
comes from a children's book. I sang it to you and now
you are passing it on to your children/nieces: *I'll love you
forever, I'll like you for always; as long as I'm living, my
darling you'll be.*

The top values I encourage for you are:

RELATIONSHIPS
Our hearts seek and desire relationship. We were made
for God and to connect with each other. Sometimes we
have such high expectations of others, especially of those
we love. Over the course of time, you will understand
that your dear ones will not be able to meet all of the
needs of your heart. Only God can love you; only He can
fill your deepest longings.

FAILURE
Failure is inevitable. The hardest failure is when you hurt
someone you love. And you will—whether by thoughtless
word or selfish action, you will hurt a dear love. The only

way to remedy the situation will be to accept what you have done, seek forgiveness from God who is merciful and begin to try with your words and actions to repair the wrong that you have committed. Time heals all wounds. Scars may remain forever. Only forgiveness diminishes scars.

WORK ETHIC
Work is constant, whether in relationships or daily life. I believe that hard work has always been exemplified to you and I believe that you know and understand that this is the way of life. Know also when to relax, know that you can only do so much and that the nature of things is that there is always more to do. Be at peace with yourself, and with God. Then what you do, will be enough.

I will love you forever,
Mom

A THOUGHT FROM THE MOM'S CORNER

"A mom's hug lasts long after she lets go."

Author Unknown

Susan Leary

Susan Leary   Born 1974
Married to Darren 11 years
1997 - BBA in Accounting,
University of Cincinnati
CAREER - CPA
HOBBIES – Anything active: hiking,
skiing, running

To my children Marisa, Connor and Tyler, ages 9, 7 and 5,

Know that: I love you with all my heart, now and always. There is nothing I would not do for you.

The top values I encourage for you are:

BALANCE
Work Hard. You will be amazed at how much you can accomplish. You are capable of much, much more than you might believe. While the easy route will take less time and energy, hard work will provide better, more satisfying opportunities. But hard work must be rewarded. Climb the tallest mountain and enjoy the view when you get to the top – it will be worth the effort.

ENJOY THE WORLD AROUND YOU
Slow down, and take the time to enjoy your surroundings. You will create a beautiful life, full of warm friendships, laughter, loving relationships, and professional successes. Take the time to experience the beauty you have created.

BE THOUGHTFUL
Listen with the intention to understand. Listening provides the chance to learn something new. Speak

powerfully, honestly, and with purpose. Say what you mean, and do what you say.

BELIEVE IN YOURSELF
You are smart. You are kind. You can do it. You can accomplish anything you set your mind to. Believe in yourself and others will to.

Love to each of you always,
Mom

A THOUGHT FROM THE MOM'S CORNER
"You never realize how much your mother loves you till you explore the attic - and find every letter you ever sent her, every finger painting, clay pot, bead necklace, Easter chicken, cardboard Santa Claus, paper lace Mother's Day card and school report since day one."

Pam Brown

Brooke Lengle

Brooke Crawford Lengle
Mother of Ella (16 months)
Wife of Scott (3 years)

Career: Elementary Teacher
BS: Northern Kentucky University-
Elementary Education
MA: University of the Cumberlands-
Reading and Writing Specialist

Hobbies: Spending time with family, hiking, gardening, cooking, reading, and camping

*T*o my Ella (16 months),

I remember tears of joy streaming down my face the first time I saw you. God had blessed your dad and I with a beautiful and healthy baby girl.

Know that: As a parent, I wish you happiness and success in all areas of your life; however, here are a few more words of wisdom to guide you through:

The top values I encourage for you are:

GOD
Have a strong faith in God. Count your blessings every day; never take anything for granted. Practice your beliefs by your actions. The power of prayer is truly miraculous. In trying times remember that God does not give us more than we can handle.

FAMILY
Your family will always be there for you in good times and bad. Take care of one another.

LOVE
In your search of choosing a partner in your life, remember to never settle for less than you deserve. Life is much more enjoyable if you find your true love to share it with.

EDUCATION
Be a lifetime learner! It is never too late to learn something new. Expand your horizons. Being well educated makes you an open-minded individual.

CAREER
Find your passion! Choose a career that you look forward to go to each day. It does not matter how much money you make, just make enough money to take care of yourself. Be a dedicated employee, come in early, stay late and work hard. Things are so much more enjoyable when you earn them.

FINANCES
Be humble. Do not spend more money than you earn. Determine needs versus wants early in life. Never try to keep up with the Jones'. You are the only one in control of your finances; make smart choices.

Life is a wonderful gift, treasure each moment. Ella, I am proud to call you my daughter. I wish you all the happiness and success in the world.

I love you,

Mom

Dolores (Dee) Lorenz

Dolores (Dee) Lorenz - Born: 1951
Married to Dr. Bob Lorenz for 40 years
Bishop Brossart High School (Alexandria, Ky.)
Good Samaritan Hospital School of Nursing (Cincinnati, Oh) – Registered Nurse - 41years
Present Volunteer Positions:
Parish Nurse and Coordinator for St. Thomas Parish Health Ministry (Ft. Thomas, Ky.)
St. Elizabeth Hospice Unit (Ft. Thomas, Ky.)
Hobbies: Bicycling, Hiking, Walking, Reading

To my son, Rob (age 35), my daughter Katie (age 32), her husband Chris Courtney (age 32), and my beautiful grandchildren – Ben (age 3) and Cara (age 1),

Know that: Your Dad and I love you so very much. You are the greatest joy and blessing in our lives, and we are so proud of each one of you. I have learned so much from you. Our parents, family, teachers, friends, co-workers, and all those we meet along the way, influence our lives and help mold us into the people we are today. We learn constantly from one another. All the events of my life (the good, the bad, and the ugly) have made me who I am today. Life is a journey – our preparation for Eternal Life – which is the GOAL! The following are the most important life lessons that I have learned on my journey thus far, and I would like to share them with you and encourage you to consider them.

PRAY EVERY DAY
Prayer changes things. It gives us strength and courage. When you lift up your praise, thanksgiving, thoughts, words and actions to God, and take Him with you through the day, you will never face a hopeless situation.

ALWAYS DO THE "RIGHT GOOD THING"
Do everything out of love for God and others. Never compromise what you know in your heart is right, just to please someone else.

MAKE TIME TO VOLUNTEER AND BE OF SERVICE
All you need to serve is a heart full of love. It will bring
MUCH joy to your life and to the lives of those you touch.

TAKE RESPONSIBILITY FOR YOUR OWN CHOICES
Be truthful, respectful, and sincere. We must recognize
the dignity of each person, and not be judgmental.
Always remember that happiness comes from within. We
alone are responsible for our emotions, feelings, attitude,
and the way we behave. Attitude checks now and then
can keep us on track.

ACTIONS SPEAK LOUDER THAN WORDS
Always be a good example. Children will follow your lead.
Be cheerful, smile, and laugh. A sense of humor is a
wonderful thing! Always be positive. Negativity breeds
hopelessness. Be good to others, love one another, and
obey the commandments.

MAKE A DIFFERENCE IN THE LIVES OF PEOPLE
It could be as simple as a smile and cheerful greeting to a
passerby; a helping hand to a harried mother; a meal or a
visit to the homebound; giving a ride to church or the
grocery; a nursing home visit or card to a lonely elderly
person. Be a good listener.

BE FORGIVING
Take the first step to forgive. Forgiving someone is the
highest and most beautiful form of love. Unforgiveness
breeds anger and hatred – never a good thing. Don't
forget to forgive yourself! We all make mistakes in life.
They help to form us. Hopefully we learn something from
each one.

May you share your gifts and talents generously. May
you be sincere in your love, cheerful in your work, and
patient in your troubles. Stay close to the Lord always.
May God bless you.

Mom/ Grandma

Lynn Mark

Lynn Mark   Born: 1951
Married to Leonard for 38 years
Education:
Clark University: BA Psychology
University of Connecticut: Masters
 in Counseling
University of Cincinnati: Masters in
Graduate Studies
Careers: Vocational Rehabilitation
Counselor for people with
disabilities, career counselor,
research associate.
Hobbies: ballroom dancing, fitness,
art history

To my three sons, Charley (age 32), Jeremy (age 29) and David (age 29),

Know that: You and Dad are the loves of my life. You should be proud of the fine men you have become and your accomplishments. You have strong commitment to family and friends; you live your lives with honesty, integrity and genuine concern for other people.

The top values that I encouraged for you are:

RELATIONSHIPS
Always treasure your relationships and be committed to your family and friends. Communication is the key to relationships, especially in a marriage. Not everything is important, so select your battles carefully. Meaningful relationships require your attention, nurturing, and coming to a consensus. I hope you will work hard to develop relationships and be rewarded with special lifelong friends.

PARENTING
Parenting is a joyful, but most daunting and humbling task. No one is a perfect parent, but you do the very best you can do at that point in time with the resources available to you. After having children of my own, I

realize they learn their values from the little everyday actions, not big speeches. It is essential for you to be available when your children want to talk. They will ask the most important life questions while you are waiting on a checkout line or other seemingly inopportune times. Make time every day to eat together with your children without distractions of phones, computers or TV. Their conversations may involve a grunt of bare acknowledgement or result in deep conversations.

I regret that I sometimes took parenting too seriously. Learn to laugh at the "disasters." If you can't laugh at the time, eventually (maybe many years later) the situations will be funny and will become wonderful stories to share with your children.

LIFELONG LEARNING

I am grateful that you have taken your education seriously and are using your education to try to better the world for other people. Learning is a lifelong pursuit taking many forms. Of course study and reading are important, but learning from relationships, experiences, and the beauty of the arts and nature add depth to our understanding. Find your passions in life and pursue them.

SOCIAL JUSTICE

One of the best things you can do with your life is to make this world a little bit better place. When I think of social justice, I think of the Hebrew word "tzedakah," meaning justice and fairness, not simply charity.

As your grandma Vita exemplified, find the people or issues that may be overlooked. Then be generous in contributing your time, talents and money to aim for the highest level of tzedakah: enabling the recipient to become self-sufficient.

All my love,
Mom

Janet Marsh

Janet GH Marsh and her husband, Ken, live on a lovely lake in the foothills of South Carolina. Both are natives of the Northeast, with some years in the Midwest. Son Paul, age 50, lives in Stamford, CT with his wife and two sons. Son Abe, age 32, lives in Piedmont, SC with his wife. Janet received her PhD from the University of Chicago in 1994 in social welfare policy. During her 40-year career she engaged in advocacy and organizing, administration, research and teaching in the social welfare field. Happily retired, she enjoys traveling, working with organizations including her church, hiking, water sports, knitting and reading.

To my sons Paul and Abe,

Know that: being your mother is my most satisfying life experience. I love you both, so very much. To my great joy, we share many values. You have known much of what I am writing from an early age. By putting my values on paper, however, I am giving you a written legacy that affirms that we, as mother and sons, are on similar paths as we move through our lives, singly and together. The source of my values is the Golden Rule: *Do onto others, as you would have them do unto you.* Universal and inclusive, it is a central belief in all major spiritual paths. It is a simple concept to understand. As guidance for living, however, it is truly difficult, in part because it embodies so many other values, values such as care for ourselves and acceptance of others.

The top values I encourage for you are:

CARE FOR YOURSELF

Look inward to nourish yourself ... your soul. Emotional and spiritual needs may sometimes be drowned out by the practicalities of everyday living but herein can be your greatest joy. Take time to know yourselves, not at the level defined by the world which encourages aggrandizement of ego, but at your deepest, least defined level - your soul.

Openness to new ways of thinking is essential for a fulfilling life and for being a good citizen of the world. I have not known either of you to hold ideas only because they reinforce your sense of self; don't let older age change that. Attending to your physical needs is a given, but too often only important in later years. Eat, drink, sleep, and move with appreciation for the miracle of your body. Listen to it - what is the ache in your shoulder saying; the recurring headache? You are your best when you feel good - spiritually, emotionally and physically! You are your best when you accept and care for yourself just as you are – not perfect but on the path.

CARE FOR OTHERS

Technology gives us more and more information – much of it troubling to our peace of mind. It is easy to stereotype and label people and ideas with which you are unfamiliar or predisposed to fear or dislike. Should you take the easy route and accept the stereotypes or just turn yourself off?
I believe we are in this world to serve one another – not to revel in conspicuous consumption or climb the career ladder at all costs. We are all part of one universal field of energy – what happens to one affects all. As economic recessions, natural disasters, and wars show us, there is a fine line between "us" and "them."
I hope you feel good when you know food, health care, income assistance are reaching people who so desperately need these supports, domestically or internationally. I hope you feel good when a news report shows that empowered citizens are demanding their rights, sometimes against US interests.
In her book *Twelve Steps to a Compassionate Life* Karen Armstrong encourages readers to "make a place for the other." To do this, first be aware of your thoughts. If negative or dismissive, try to make a space in your mind for more information, for more empathy. I know of no other way to reverse the trend toward the exclusion of the other – whether people or ideas – which is causing untold and unnecessary suffering across the world. Do you risk being called a "do-gooder?" Probably, but do you really want to be called a "do-bader?"

There are so many poignant quotes with which to conclude; I have loved this one over many years.
"Live simply that others may simply live." Elizabeth Seton

Much love, Mom

Andrea McCartney

Andrea McCartney (nee Howard)
Born 1979
Married to David McCartney for 4 years
2002 – BKin from McMaster University in Hamilton, Ontario CANADA
2004 – MScOT from University of Toronto
CAREER - Occupational Therapist
Loves sports, travel, cottage country, dinners out!

To my sons Owen (3) and Connor (10 months),

Know that: Your father and I are loving watching your smiling faces everyday – this age is so special – you are growing and learning so much everyday! We love you so much! I write this thinking about the lessons I want to teach you as you grow up, but I realize they are the lessons I value most important from my own upbringing by your grandparents Grammy and D-Dad. I hope I can teach you without even knowing I'm giving you a lesson – just like they did!

The top values I encourage for you are:

BE THE CHANGE YOU WISH TO SEE
As you grow up, you will see so many opportunities for change. Maybe you don't like something the way it is, maybe you will see a new opportunity, maybe you have a great idea….whatever it is, make it happen. Too often we sit back, don't follow through with ideas or complain about situations without doing anything about it. Be the change; make it happen.

DON'T LET THE CHALLENGE BECOME THE EXCUSE
Many things you will do will be difficult. You'll fail a couple of times; you'll encounter roadblocks and difficult people. Just because something is hard, doesn't mean you should give up.

TELL PEOPLE THEY ARE DOING A GOOD JOB
It is very easy to tell people when they are doing
something wrong. While giving *and* receiving constructive
criticism is a very important skill in life, it is also
important to tell people when they are doing a good job.
Whether it is a friend, a coworker or a stranger, you will
not believe what happiness you can bring to someone by
acknowledging his or her good work.

TO DECREASE ANXIETY, USE THE RULE OF 5
When you feel like getting mad, you are angry or feeling
anxious about a situation, use the rule of 5. Will this
matter 5 minutes from now? 5 weeks from now? 5
months from now? 5 years from now? If it won't matter,
let it go. It is so hard to let go of anger, to walk away
and be the bigger person. I guarantee you will be
healthier and happier if you follow this rule!

WORK TO KEEP YOUR FRIENDS AND FAMILY CLOSE
You won't be able to stay friends with everyone, and you
won't be able to be close with all your family members,
but strive to keep them. This takes work. You will have
to travel out of your way, forgive and forget, host
get-to-gethers and call someone who just doesn't seem to
have time to call you. People will come and go out of
your life, but put the effort in to keep your loved ones
close. These relationships are central to who you are as a
person! You'll miss them when they are gone.

With All my Love,
Mommy

Mary Jo McCartney

Mary Jo McCartney was born in 1947 in Toronto, Ontario, Canada.
She lived in St. Catharines, Ontario and was educated at schools in St. Catharines, Toronto, and Windsor. She is the mother of five sons and grandmother of eight, soon to be ten. She spent thirty-two very happy years teaching Kindergarten to Grade 3 in Toronto and Markham, Ontario.
Her special interests are family activities of any kind, music, sports, walking, travel, and reading.

To my sons: Ryan, Andrew, Matthew, Justin, and David,

Know that: I love you more than you will ever know. You have brought incredible joy into my life and I thank God every day that you were part of His plan for me. You have grown from tumbledown, fun-loving, little boys into confident, adventurous, caring adults, and I am so proud of you. Your spouses are beautiful, loving women who have become my beloved girls and your children are the perfect answer to all my dreams of being a grandmother.

My prayer for you each day is this:

BE TRUE TO YOURSELF AND YOUR FAMILY

Cherish the gift of your family. Therein is found your legacy to the future. Be patient. Be understanding. Be respectful. Listen well. Rejoice together in times of achievement, big or small. Encourage and hold one another up in times of difficulty. Stay close. Enjoy the ordinary, everyday happenings that make up your day. Share your hopes and your dreams. Walk the path that makes you a loving, thoughtful, supportive partner, parent, and sibling. 'People will forget what you said, forget what you did, but will never forget how you made them feel' (Maya Angelou). Your family is your most valuable asset and everlasting treasure. All other things are merely *things* and, in the end, will mean nothing to anyone. But, the world will be a better place because you were a person of integrity and you were important in the lives of your family.

BE LOVING

Remember that stones can build walls or build bridges. You have learned that life can bring unexpected challenges. You have faced these challenges and have learned so much in the process. May you always be brave and strong in the face of adversity. Unconditional love is one of life's most important gifts.

BE FAITH-FILLED

Pray often. Pray for one another. Be thankful. You have been greatly blessed. God is always with you.

BE WISE

Choose your friends and associates carefully, remembering that no one is perfect. Everyone comes with a history of their own. Accept that others may see life differently. Be tolerant. Try to see through their eyes. Have a kind and loving heart that is quick to forgive and ask for forgiveness.

BE GENEROUS

Celebrate the many blessings you have received and continue to bless others by giving back whenever and wherever you find the opportunity. Volunteer your time. Give to worthy causes. Become a blood donor. Everything you do will make a difference.

BE HAPPY, WEAR A SMILE, AND LAUGH TOGETHER

Find happiness in every day. Be optimistic. Be positive. Have fun and learn to laugh at yourself. After all, "A smile is an inexpensive way to improve your looks."

You are the gift that keeps on giving to me. I pray for you and your families every day. May you always remember how much you are loved and treasured.

Loving you forever and for always,
Mom

Pam McLaughlin

Pam McLaughlin
Married to Michael for 28 Years
My husband's work has taken us many places, Colorado, Omaha, San Diego, Cincinnati, and recently The East Bay, 45 minutes outside San Francisco. Each move has given me the opportunity to try new things, meet new people and make life long friends.
My passion besides my family is fitness and volunteering.
I am a certified fitness instructor and I use my knowledge to guide my family to healthy living. Two personal accomplishments that make me proud are running a marathon and rappelling down a cavern.
Volunteer- I have volunteered or helped raise money for the Symphony, Orchestra, Zoo, Sacred Heart, Catholic Charities, Athletic Boosters, Girl Scouts, PTA's, and local schools. My new project is becoming a volunteer for the American Red Cross helping with disaster relief and blood services.

To my Children Jennifer (25), Melanie (23), Joseph (22), Kyle (16),

Know that: I have wanted to be a mom since I can remember. While most of my friends were busy choosing a career path and climbing the corporate ladder, I occupied my time contemplating how many children I would have and what their names would be. My goal in life was to be the" best" mom; my priority was my family and my "job" became my home. I hope I haven't let you down.
When life becomes rough and you feel like nothing is going right, I hope you will remember "Mom's Motto." In case you forgot here is a reminder: Be Safe, Be Honest, Be Good, Be Kind, Be True, Be Brave and Have Faith.

The top values I encourage for you are:

HAVE FAITH
Faith will be tested, as we know. Believe that there is a place beyond the clouds with a guardian watching over you and giving you the strength you need to go on when friends, family, job or life has let you down.

BE HONEST
Whenever your back is up against the wall, or you see an injustice, be honest with yourself and the people around you. Love unconditionally- do not put conditions on the people you love. The one fault we have is free will. With free will, we will disappoint the people we love and they will disappoint us. Learn to forgive and love without condition.

BE BRAVE
Don't be afraid to turn your back on the ocean! A wave will knock you down as will life. Get up, dust off the sand then turn around and dive in! You will feel much better not knowing the strength of the wave and rejoice at knowing it didn't beat you.

BE GOOD
Live a good life! Be a good friend, neighbor, sister, brother, aunt, uncle, daughter, son, husband or wife.
Be Kind- Look out for one another and be kind to the people around you.

BE SAFE
Always be prepared for the unexpected in any situation. Think, what if..........

BE TRUE
Be true to yourself. Don't settle; know what you are made of, know your limits, and know your strengths. When you're ready to reach for a star go for it and when it's not what you want, say "I am content" and walk away.

I hope that I have given you the tools you need to be successful, respectable, responsible, kind and caring adults. It is also my hope that, as the years go by, I continue to learn from you as you have taught me so much. Jennifer, you have taught me the depths of integrity; Melanie, the meaning of unconditional love; Joe, the strength of courage and hope; and Kyle, you have taught me the meaning of acceptance.

Even though I've spent most of my life planning to be a mom, nothing prepared me for the joy and overwhelming love I felt when I brought each of you into this world.

I LOVE YOU MORE.
Mom

Jennifer P. Mearns

Jennifer Mearns
BS: Bryant University (Smithfield, RI);
served as Vice Chair of Board of Trustees.
CAREER PATH- PR Assistant at Madison
Square Garden; Media Liaison for Men's
Professional Tour; partner in global Sports
Marketing agency; owner of Executive
Recruiting/Talent Acquisition consulting
firm;
Northern Kentucky University First Lady.
HOBBIES – running, hiking, reading and
spending time with friends and family.

To my beautiful children, Bridget, Christina, Clare, Geoffrey, and Molly,

Know that: You have brought me more joy than I ever imagined. You make me laugh with your quick humor and interesting everyday observations. You also challenge me on occasion. But you always bring me pure joy.

I am very proud of each of you. Despite coming from a large family of five kids, you are all unique and different. You share common values and traits, and yet you are very much each your own person and are comfortable with who you are. You haven't let the big family swallow you up and mold you. You've each taken your own different and interesting path to find your own fulfillment. I am very proud of you for doing that.

The top values I encourage for you are:

HAPPINESS
Mostly, what I want for you is to be truly happy. Happiness has to come from within, and then it can be shared with others. Looking to others to make your happiness creates resentment and disappointment. Be happy with yourselves and be able to share that happiness with others.

EDUCATION
Take full advantage of the educational opportunities being offered to you. Your grandparents instilled the value of education in us when we were growing up. Grander was the first in his family to go to college. When he had children, six out of nine ended up earning masters or JD degrees. Grandpa Proud didn't have the opportunity to go to college. He had to go straight to work to help support his family. So my siblings and I were first-generation college students and it opened our world to so many opportunities. We continue to encourage you to really get everything you can out of your education and not just show up, but to really immerse yourself and get involved.

TAKING RISKS
As you go out into the world, don't be afraid to take risks, to try different things. Keep your mind open to new opportunities, new cultures, and new ways of thinking. Do not be afraid to make mistakes. Learn and grow, taking advantage of every opportunity that presents itself.

SERVING OTHERS
You all have been volunteering for most of your lives, sometimes by force, many times by choice. I hope you continue to make time to volunteer and serve the community. Find something that you are really passionate about, and commit your time and resources to help others.

All my love,

Mom

Mary Mickelson

Mary Mickelson
Born in San Diego, BS in nursing from San Diego State University, married 48 years to my loving husband, Phil. Public health nurse. Later, part owner of a homecare company in San Diego. My children:
Tina, a teaching golf pro; Philip, a professional golf pro; and Timmy, a golf coach at ASU (Arizona State University)
My hobbies are sports with basketball as my favorite.

To my three children: Tina, Philip, and Timmy,

Know that: the eternal love we have for you is so complete. And now we see it in your children. You are wonderful parents and, sometimes, we wish we had done things that you are doing today. Your children are fortunate to have you for parents, and dad and I get the benefits of having outstanding grandchildren.

From the time that you were born and arrived into this world, each of you had your own distinct personalities that followed you to the present day. You are all strong leaders.

Tina, you are always so calm and patient, so loving and agreeable. I see that in your children and how you are passing that on to them.

Philip, you are very independent, very caring and strong. We noticed from an early age how focused you were with anything that was important to you, and now we see that, not only in your golf, but in your family and how important they are to you.

Timmy, you are a great combination of both Tina and Philip. You kind of went with the flow. Their gymnastics and their golf were always so important, and I'd wake you up from the middle of an afternoon nap, when they came home from school, and we would pop you into the front seat. Tina would lean over in our little Volkswagen bug and pop a bottle in your mouth as we drove to gymnastics and then to golf. You would try to get a little nap and then we had to wake you up again to go and pick them up. I think that helped with your development. You are very responsible and have always been able to adjust. You have a deep concern for others and are always willing to help. You make a terrific golf coach.

You are all very strong individuals, and thank goodness you are very athletic with very special talents.

FAITH – FAMILY - FRIENDS
Faith: It is important that you have faith and that you be thankful everyday for your blessings.
Family: No one will ever love you more or be more supportive than your own family. The most difficult job and yet the most rewarding is being a parent. Your dad and I knew how important family is. That is why we decided that I would stay home until you were in school.
Friends: Choose them wisely, for you will be judged by your friends. Cherish them.

CONSISTENT DISCIPLINE
Be consistent with your discipline with yourself and your children. Talk things through with your family and work together. Your grandparents also stressed family: they stressed never lie nor cheat anyone. Lying should never be done; be truthful to yourself.

TALENTS
You all have special talents so use them wisely. Your talent doesn't mean that you are a better person, so treat others as you would like to have them treat you. *Be* a better person.

The most difficult and yet the most rewarding time was when you graduated. At that time we realized you would be forming your own families. We were so proud and yet so sad that we would no longer have you in our home as children.

Love, Mom

Maria Molina

Married to: Daniel Molina
Education: BA from XU
Career: Communications, Procter & Gamble
Interests: Spending time with Family and Friends, running.
Hobbies: Reading, cooking (when I have time), more recently travel!

To Yvonne, Dan, Adam and Roland,

Know that: This is a precious opportunity to share some thoughts that your Father and I have conveyed to the four of you in word and actions through the last 40 years.

The top values I encourage for you are:
WE ARE A PORTRAIT OF AMERICA
Be proud of who you are. Ours is the story of an American Dream that has come "full circle"! Your Great-Grandmother on my Dad's side was born in New Haven, CT of English-Irish immigrants; my Great-Grandparents on my Mother's side fled from the Franco regime in Spain. Your paternal Grandma was born of German-Italian immigrant parents in Louisville, KY. And all these lives came together in Havana, Cuba, where your Pops and I were born. How ironic that we would have to flee Communist Cuba as young children ourselves in the 1960's in search, once again, of personal freedoms and better opportunities! And how lucky for us that Daniel Molina and Maria Graziella Arencibia – two young Cuban political refugees from Havana -- would meet for the first time in Cincinnati, Ohio, and fall in love. What a great reminder that in every cloud there is a silver lining! The history of humanity is filled with stories like ours of triumph over adversity.

GOD DANCED THE DAY YOU WERE BORN
From the day you came into this world we've watched you blossom into the unique work of God that you are. You are our greatest Legacy. Each of you four is making this

world a better place in small and big ways by using the gifts and talents God has generously given you to be a Blessing to those around you in His name. Our hearts are full of joy and pride as we watch how each of you has taken your place in the world, at home, at work and in the communities where you work and live.

ROOTS AND WINGS
You were raised surrounded by lots of love in a modest, cape cod in Deer Park, OH. You may not have worn name brands, and we may have been a little crowded in the house, but you were millionaires where it counted. In the tradition of our Latin culture, you grew up surrounded by an extended family of grandparents, aunts and uncles and cousins – and our beloved neighbors on Myrtle Ave. Yes, you were loved and nurtured by a proverbial "Village."

BLOOM WHERE YOU ARE PLANTED or "TRANSPLANTED"
We know from our personal experience about the fleeing nature of material possessions. We have instilled in you that what will take you far in life is personal values, honesty, a strong work ethic and having an education. With these at hand, you can always begin again no matter where life takes you. We know because we did, as did our parents, grand and great-grandparents before us.

BEING YOUR MOM IS MY GREATEST ACCOMPLISHMENT!
How often have I said that we plan and then life happens? We must always be willing to make adjustments based on what life asks of us. I wanted to be a "stay-at-home" mom. You see, having had parents that divorced when I was only 5, keeping our family together has been my most important priority. In this, Pops and I have always been a team. But finances dictated that I go to work after Roland started Kindergarten. Looking back I'm so glad I did because -- as a result, I expanded professionally in into new and unexpected horizons. Yet, being your Mom will always be my greatest accomplishment and legacy.

I love ya bunches!!! Mom

Nancy Nolan

Nancy Nolan moved to Cincinnati, OH in 1985. She lives with her husband and dog Nelly in the suburb of Montgomery. She started Nolan Kerr Artists in 1996 to help young musicians develop their careers. She volunteers with the City of Montgomery Arts Commission, St. Barnabas Episcopal Church, Linden Grove School (for children on the autism spectrum), and The Assistance League of Greater Cincinnati.

To my son, Max (22), and my stepchildren Tiffany (30) and Chris (29),

Know that: When each of you came into my life, my world blossomed. It became a richer thing, a busy place full of creativity, laughter, hugs, the occasional heartbreak, but above all a haven of caring and love. You taught me about the meaning of caring for others and putting myself aside. You reminded me of the many times when I was young that my own mother showed me her gentle kindness, and how important a smile or hug or peanut butter cookie can be when you are very small in a very big universe. I wanted to give you moments of grace just like my Mom did for me. I hope I succeeded.

The top values I encourage for you are:

LOVE YOURSELF
We can't truly love God if we don't cherish our own place in the world, as one of His children. Loving yourself doesn't mean buying fancy cars or bragging about your successes or counting your Facebook friends. It's about caring for your body, mind and spirit, much as you would your own child, nurturing yourself in ways that bring you closer to the ideal God has in mind for all of us. Believe God has a plan for you in the world and do everything you can to be ready for it. Keep healthy habits, and give yourself the freedom to be happy, to take risks, and to make mistakes. Forgive yourself for your imperfections

just as God forgives. Thank God every day for the gift of your life.

FIND YOUR PASSION

There is nothing so good as sitting down to a task you enjoy and looking up, hours later, shocked at how much time has passed. Embrace those things you love to do! Nurture them, practice them, enjoy them every chance you get. Your passions for art or sports or music or writing are prized possessions that no one can take from you. They will always be there to comfort you in times of doubt or stress. As the years progress, you will continue to discover new talents within yourself, and new ways of sharing your gifts with others. Keep your eyes open to learning new things.

HAVE COMPASSION

Your Dad and I are so proud of the caring adults you have become. We rest in the certainty that all of you will be there to help those in need, and that you will never consciously do anything to hurt another. Compassion is a challenging attribute that allows us to stand in the shoes of another, to feel their sorrow or anger or shame, and to sense how to help.

Someone said about the blues that you can't really sing it if you've never suffered. Out of pain can come real joy. Use your own disappointments and hurts to inform your compassion for others. Realize that every bad or sad day you have helps to forge you into a vessel of compassion, enabling you to do the work God has called us all to do: To care for one another and to help make the world a beautiful place to be.

I thank each of you for being you, and for being in my world. It is, truly, a beautiful place to be.

Love, Mom

Margaret (Peggy) Norris

Margaret (Peggy) Norris
Born in 1952
Married to Randy Norris for 37 years
Administrative Asst. &
Religion Teacher – Holy Family School
Sacristan – St. Benedict Church
Proud Parent

*T*o my four wonderful children, Angela (36), Michael (33), Laura (30), and Tim (26),

The top values I encourage for you are:

KEEP GOD FIRST IN YOUR LIFE
Even when we make mistakes just remember that God still loves us. Talk to God on a daily basis and it's funny how those big troubles somehow seem to diminish. He loves to listen to you just the way your Mom and Dad do.

YOU GET OUT OF LIFE WHATEVER YOU PUT INTO IT
If you are constantly complaining to people --- look around to see who exactly is listening. If you don't work hard in whatever you do, then you are not really working --- you're just getting by and are you being true to yourself, then? Take pride in everything that you do and always do your best. If you do it right the first time, you won't have to redo it.

MAKE GOOD FRIENDS
Choose your friends wisely. Remember that you become the person that you hang out with. The people that you are friends with begin to influence you in all things and some choices are not necessarily the right choices.

ALWAYS BE HONEST
Be truthful in everything. Lies hurt --- not only yourself but your family and friends. Sometimes it might be hard

to tell the truth but you will feel much better about yourself in the long run.

REMEMBER THE GOLDEN RULE
"Do unto others as you would have them do unto you." Sometimes it is hard to forgive people when they've hurt us, and we keep telling ourselves that "getting back" at that person is how we want to deal with it. That's not how things should be handled.

REMEMBER YOUR FAMILY
Family should stick together. Families are the only ones who really matter. You might say to yourself "My friends are the ones who really care about me." Look, when it comes down to it, are friends in it for the long haul? Or just when it is convenient to them? Your family will provide you with unconditional love and support. Remember to love your family back!!!

Life is an adventure – enjoy it.

Love and Kisses and Big Bear Hugs,
Mom

A THOUGHT FROM THE MOM'S CORNER
"Let France have good mothers, and she will have good sons."

Napoleon Bonaparte

Julie O'Neill

When Julie's not anchoring the weekend evening news or chasing a big story as a member of Cincinnati's WCPO-TV's revered I-Team investigative unit, she's chasing her two children ("G-boy" and "Sam E.") and a dog named "Blue"... and she's probably singing show tunes while she's at it. She comes from a family of opera singers and concert pianists, and studied Musical Theatre at the University of Cincinnati's prestigious College Conservatory of Music.
Julie received her Broadcast Journalism degree from Louisiana State University and notes two career "moments" that stand out: the interview with Mother Teresa and the day she spilled coffee on President Clinton (he wasn't badly hurt).

To my 7 year-old daughter, Samantha, and my 11-year old son, Garrett,

Know that: Since you, Garrett, were little I have often asked you what you think I love about you the most. And you always answered, "My beautiful loving heart." You know...and now Samantha knows, that your hearts are what set you apart and the way you show love to others is what makes me most proud of you both.

GOOD MINDSET
Sure, you both are funny, charming, talented, good-looking etc. And I tell you that, but when trying to lift you up, I try to focus on behaviors I want to encourage. As you get older, I want you to be in tune with what's going on inside the people around you and so I say things like, "I love to see how you're developing into a person who is looking for ways to lift others up and serving people in need. It shows what a beautiful heart you have." I believe that mindset, more than anything, will equip you to have strong, loving relationships that will bring you happiness and fulfillment.

PURSUE YOUR DREAMS WITH CONFIDENCE

I want you to know that you are loved, by God and by your family, and you are precious and unique and have a special purpose in life. I want you to believe in yourselves and pursue your dreams and desires, but also to know your joy in life will come from staying rooted in and connected to your calling and purpose. I also want you to have complete confidence that I will always be there for you. When I see you feeling a bit insecure or afraid, I remind you that I am Mother Eagle and ask if you remember what Mother Eagle will do if anyone tries to harm her baby eaglets. You laugh and roll your eyes a bit and say, "Claw their eyes out!"

GOOD TRADITIONS

I was told long ago the best time to have a real conversation with a child is at bedtime (when they'll do anything to get out of going to sleep). When I pray with you at night, we ask the Lord to show us how to be better servants for Him. We also give thanks for all our circumstances, good and bad. We talk about how the good circumstances bring us joy and validation...and the bad circumstances bring us opportunities...for increased faith or important emotional growth. We talk about the good and bad of the day...and then I tell you "Super Sam" and "Super Garrett" bedtime stories. Of course the stories always end with Samantha or Garrett saving the day, and it was usually because you used your brains or creativity to find the solution. My dad always told me "Super De De" stories (my nickname) and I loved ending the day that way. It's been a great tradition to pass on.

All my love, Mom

Robin Quallick

Robin Quallick - Born: 1985
Married to Jeff Quallick for 2 years
Campbell County High (Alexandria, Ky.)
Northern KY University: Recreational Fitness
RUSH: Mgr – Stay at Home Mother
Hobbies: Pinterest, Crafts, Home
improvements, Baking, dogs (Sophie &
Jangles)

To my son Benjamin who will be born in March of 2014,

Know that: My entry to you will be a bit different from the other mom's pages, because unlike them, I am still waiting to meet you. The things that I am about to discuss are things that I hope your dad and I are able to instill in you as you grow.

BE GRATEFUL
Be grateful for the things you have, while working for the things you want. You will have a lot to be thankful for: Your health, your family, your friends, your home, and many more. While you may be wishing for the things that you don't have, someone out there may be wishing they had what you already have. Every breath is a gift from God, so be thankful that He has chosen to bless you with another day to enjoy the gift of life.

KEEP GOD IN YOUR LIFE
Keep God in your life and pray often. Pray for yourself and pray for others. Pray that God gives you the courage to be the man that He has intended for you to be. Don't just talk to God, but also listen to what He has to say.

ALWAYS GIVE 110%
Always give 110% of yourself, no matter how big or small the task. Push yourself to always be better than the last time. Never avoid something because you are afraid to fail. You miss 100% of the shots you don't take.

READ YOUR BIBLE OFTEN
Read your Bible and read it often. The Bible is bread for daily use, not cake for special occasions. Pray before and after you read it. Pray that God speaks to you through His word, and pray that you interpret His word in the way He intended.

SMELL THE ROSES
Stop to smell the roses from time to time. Watch the sun rise and set. There is beauty all round you. God is a truly amazing artist!

BE THANKFUL
Always be grateful as well as gracious when someone gives you a gift. No matter how big or small, no one owes you anything; so when they have taken time to think of you, show gratitude.

DO WHAT IS RIGHT
Always do what is right, even if it is not popular.

DIY
Learn to be handy. You'd be surprised how much money you can save and how much satisfaction you receive just by using a little elbow grease.

LAUGH
Laugh often, and don't be afraid to laugh at yourself.

BE KIND
Be kind and serve others without expecting anything in return. Be kind, even when others are not kind to you. People may not always remember you or what you say, but they will always remember the way you made them feel.

SEE THE GOOD
Train yourself to see the good in everything. Every day may not be good, but there is something good in every day.

EDUCATION
Get the best education possible. No matter what the world takes from you, it cannot take away your education. Never stop learning. Read as many books as you can get your hands on. Read the newspaper and keep up with current events.

TRAVEL
Go anywhere and everywhere. Seek out opportunities to see the world. There is a lot of beauty out there waiting for you to discover and endless adventures for you to experience.

I'll love you forever,
Mom

Jessica Rassette

Jessica is a mom to three feisty boys in Nebraska.
She is a writer and photographer, weaving together words and photos on her blog Little Victories with Bub and Teebs. In the midst of the loveable chaos of her sons and her husband, Jessica considers herself the coordinator of these very high-energy men and wouldn't have it any other way.

My Boys,

What I want for you most in life is happiness. Whatever it is that makes you happy, I want you to do it. It is my hope for you that your happiness comes from helping others, and whether you are a doctor or artist or garbage collector I want you to recognize that what you do with this life, what you put into this world, is for the joy of others. If you can do that, if you can give freely and passionately with whatever gifts you have, happiness will find you. You don't ever need to seek happiness. Live your life well and happiness will seek *you*.

I want you to be prepared to fail. I want you to embrace it. Boys, there is so much beauty in failure. You won't always be the best or the most successful. Sometimes you'll fail so hard you will wonder how you will ever get up again. But you will. You will always get up just one time more than you fall. And that is simply beautiful.

Your life and your happiness are going to surprise you. The things you succeed at will shock you, and the things you fail at will oftentimes blindside you. But whether you are high on a mountain of success or wallowing in a valley of failure, I don't want you to take yourself too seriously. You should laugh as often as you can. Don't ever forget these deep, gurgling, boisterous giggles that erupt from your little boy bellies. If you ever want to know what success really sounds like, I can tell you that *that* is it.

Some of my favorite moments of mothering you, have been those moments of wild boyish laughter. Don't ever stop brewing that laughter so freely. And while I cherish those warm, happy moments with you, it is also the challenging times that I love just as much. The times when your tantrums tested my sanity or your strong wills made me question everything I knew about myself. It is these challenging times that taught me the things that I am now able to teach you.

Lastly, whoever you become I want you to treat everyone well. Be respectful, be courteous, and mind your manners. Remember that everyone you meet matters. If you can do that, I will feel like I've done my job.

Above all else, I want you to know that you are loved. Whatever you do, you always are loved. When failure, success, happiness, laughter, frustration all find you-- still, you are loved.

You will grow, you will leave me, you will explore. You will stretch your imaginations with the biggest of dreams. But always, you are my boys, and already I can't wait to see what you give back to the world.

Love,

Your Mama

Tracy Roblero

Tracy Roblero
Born 1979 in Cincinnati, OH
Married to Jeu for 8 years
2002 - BS, Environmental Sciences,
University Of Cincinnati
2004 - MPI, Urban Planning, Indiana
University Purdue University Indianapolis
CAREER - Mother of three wonderful
children, City Planner - City of
Montgomery, OH
HOBBIES – Spending time with my
children & family, reading & traveling

*T*o my amazing children, Isabela (7), Julianna (4) and Levi (1.5),

Know that: My love for each of you is immeasurable, indescribable and unconditional. You bring me so much joy and make me a better person. I love being your mother more than anything else in this world.

Isabela: My sweet girl, when you came into this world, everything changed for the better. You taught me the true meaning of unconditional love, how to be selfless, to be patient, to love every moment of life, and to truly appreciate my own parents. You have a kind heart and sense of humor that will take you far in this life.

Julianna: People say that I am strong, but they are wrong, you are strong. Any strength I have, any perseverance I have, comes from you. Your bravery, your strength and your courage inspire me every day. You've already faced so much in your young life and I know there is nothing that could ever stand in your way.

Levi: My little man, you gave me hope when I needed it most. You taught me that no matter how bleak life seems, good things are just around the corner. Your pure unadulterated love of life is contagious; never lose that. I am proud to call you my son and can't wait to see the man you turn out to be!

The top values I encourage for you are:

COUNT YOUR BLESSINGS
You all know first-hand how hard life can be, but you also know how wonderful it can be. When times get tough remember to count your blessings, don't borrow trouble and choose to be happy. Life will throw curveballs at you, but only you can decide what to make of them. No matter how hard it seems, don't let it bring you down. Focus on the blessings you have and all the love that surrounds you.

DON'T SWEAT THE SMALL STUFF
Remember what is important in life and don't focus on the small stuff. Keep things in perspective and don't take things personally. School, a career, and friends are important, but family trumps it all. Be kind to each other and stay close to your family; they are the only ones who are forever on your side through thick and thin.

LOVE
Be picky when it comes to giving your heart to someone. Don't compromise who you are. You are worthy of love just the way you are. I hope that you are strong enough to move on if it isn't right and are wise enough to know when it is. When you do find that forever partner, be kind to him/her. Relationships can be hard, but remember why you fell in love in the first place.

I will leave you with a few of the lyrics from a song that I love and have sung to you all your life, called "In My Daughter's Eyes" by Martina McBride. Of course I changed the lyrics to "in my child's eyes" because I see it in Levi's eyes too, girls: "This miracle God gave to me, gives me strength when I am weak, I find reason to believe, in my child's eyes."

I hope that I am half the mother to you that my mother was to me. I love you with all my heart and more,
Mom

Courtney Rubin

Courtney Rubin is a stay at home mom who loves to write about life's simple (and crazy) moments with her three young children, ages 2, 6 and 7. Her blog entitled 'Embracing The Insanity' has provided her with a way to memorialize all of the special moments she experiences with her kids. She is a life-long Florida State University Seminoles fan and a graduate of the FSU College of Law. In her spare time, she enjoys being involved with children's charities.

To my children Michael, Zoe, and Troy,

Know that: Being your mother is the greatest honor that God could have bestowed upon me. While it hasn't always been easy, I can't imagine my life without you. You bring me the greatest joy a person can have, even when you are little stinkers. You are all still young right now and I know we have quite a journey ahead of us. But I want you to know that I will always love you and will always be available to hold you and snuggle you no matter how big you get. I thank God daily for each of you.

If I can leave you with nothing else, please remember these things:

LEARN FROM YOUR MISTAKES AND FORGIVE OTHERS FOR THEIRS

No one is perfect, not even your dear old mom, as much as it pains me to admit. We all make mistakes even when our intentions stem from a pure place. Disappointments are inevitable and heartaches will occur. Despite this fact, try to look at every point in your life as a time to learn. If you make a mistake, remember it and try not to do it again. If someone else hurts you, don't hold on to the anger; forgive. Anger towards others will only hurt you. But, when you forgive, remember that moment as well, and do your best not to put yourself in the same situation again. Each moment in your life has a purpose and will make you the person that you ultimately become. Choose wisely.

BE THANKFUL AND CHARITABLE
While we are not rich, you are abundantly blessed. Even during the times when your life may seem difficult, there are always others out there having a harder time. Always be thankful for what you have and share your blessings with others. A grateful and compassionate heart is a gift to yourself and to those around you. You never know how much the smallest act of kindness can mean to someone.

LAUGH OFTEN
Life is tough. There will be things that I cannot shelter you from, as much as I will want to. To survive, you must keep a sense of humor about you. While things may not seem funny at the time, if you can learn to laugh about them later, you will heal much faster. Try to step back from the situations where you feel like nothing is going right and find hilarity in the mundane. Trust me, even in the worst of times, there will be funny moments and those are the ones to cling to when everything else goes awry. (That reminds me, I have some potty training stories to share with you when you get a little older.)

ALWAYS CALL YOUR MOTHER
I'd like to think that this one is self-explanatory, but we have yet to reach your teenage years, so I'm throwing it into this list just to be safe. I want you to know that you can always count on me no matter what might happen in your life. Please take the time to include me in the happy and the sad. Nothing makes me happier than when you come up and give me a hug or say, "I love you." I hope you will always want to do this, even when we may disagree. I will never run out of hugs for you and I will always be just a call away. SO CALL YOUR MOTHER.

I love you all the way around the world and back again.
~Mommy

Perry Schaible

Perry Schaible joined the LOCAL 12 news team in June 2010 as the Alert Desk reporter for Local 12 Good Morning Cincinnati. Today she is a morning beat reporter.

A lifelong Cincinnatian, Perry graduated from McAuley High School in College Hill before heading to Oxford, Ohio to attend Miami University where she majored in Communications.

*T*o my three smart, beautiful girls: Caroline (10), Grace (7), and Natalie (4),

"I think you're wonderful. I think you're marvelous. I think you're beautiful, and magical and filled with curiosity.... and dreams."

- Debbie Clement

Know that: I love you with all of my heart. You amaze me every day with your kindness, generosity, intrigue, and drive. The three of you have taught me how to love unconditionally and how to appreciate the different characteristics each of you possess:

Caroline, we all know you love to be "the boss," but underneath that tough outer shell you are kind and compassionate – a true nurturer. I love to watch you comfort and care for your sisters when they need a shoulder to cry on or someone to sleep with. You are the ultimate "Big Sister!" You are beautiful, smart, and kind.

Gracie, you remind me a lot of myself. You love to be the center of attention and get a laugh – the typical middle child! You are always cool as a cucumber and smart. Sometimes you amaze me with your intelligence. Your spunk is contagious. People love being around you with your positive spirit. I love when you break into song and we have our own little musical. Never let go of that bubbling personality and ALWAYS keep the smile on your face.

Natalie, the "baby" of the family who has never known she is the baby. You have been moving since the day you were born -- always full of love, 'nuggles, and spunk. I love how caring and concerned you are about your sisters and how you wait anxiously for them to come home from school. You are so smart and inquisitive.

The top values I encourage for you are:
LIVING YOUR DREAM
I cannot wait to see what kind of young ladies the three of you become as you continue to grow. Remember, you can be anything you want to be. Never let someone else discourage or stop you from living your dream, however far-fetched it may be. Always be patient and kind. You never know what situation will present itself or whom it will come through.

SUCCESS
Life is a tangled web of ups and downs, but the ultimate goal is to attain your own personal success. Success is how you view it: a goal on the soccer field or a basket on the court. Success is completing high school and then college or building a career that you love. It doesn't matter if you work as a hairdresser or a lawyer – if you give it 100 percent all the time AND you love it = SUCCESS.

GIFTS
You have given me many gifts in the last ten years: the gift of unconditional love, trust, and faith. But, best of all, you gave me the one gift only the three of you could...the gift of Motherhood. It's been an amazing ride. I can't wait to see what the future holds.

Love ya much!
Your "Mom," "Mother," and "Mudder"

Natalie Verkamp Schoeny

Natalie Verkamp Schoeny
Married to Mike for 45 years
My experience before real estate was work at a design company and 5years at Summit Country Day School ('88-93) as the Alumni Director where my 3 oldest and I graduated from. Grew up on a working farm till age 11. Catholic schools all my life. Still very involved in church activities: Jr. League projects, volunteering, member of RED Cross Tiffany Circle, Dress for Success etc.

To my wonderful sons and daughters, Rick, Mike, Michelle, Dorrie, and P.J., who are between the ages of 31 and 44,

Know that: Life's journey goes so quickly and my recollections go from the baby of the family of five children to now the mother of five children and grandmother of eleven grandchildren with more on the way.

My memories of my time as a child formed how I have viewed and related to my offspring and their offspring. I have always believed that children are in need of models not critics. As a young twenty-something mom, with my first three children born within sixteen months (you, Michelle, my daughter and then you, Mike and Rick – my premature twins).

I tried to demonstrate the love I had been shown as a child even though I was overwhelmed by the numbers. Your father helped when he was not working, but the daily responsibilities became my life. Help from your grandparents was rarely available, so I was fortunate to have a friend from Children's Hospital, whom I hired to help maintain my sanity. Dorrie and P.J., you were born 10 – 13 years later, when I was a more relaxed thirty-something mom with welcomed help from the older children. As a family of seven, we all endured the joy and challenges as a unit and drew strength and character from each other.

School, work, career, weddings, and grandchildren followed quickly. Initially, working at the children's school helped me transition to an even greater commitment; a real estate career developed my negotiating and people skills.

As a mother and grandmother, I continue to learn from you and your children's diverse views of ways and techniques of living in the now. I have been blessed from having all of you in my life. Those blessings must be shared in order to improve our world that has been brilliantly created and recreated by God, the creator.

Motherhood is something I stumbled upon but have found a deepest gratification in my journey.

The top values I encourage for you are:

LIVE LIFE TO ITS FULLEST
I continued to treat you and your children with the advice of being themselves, taking risks when you are told "you can't, or you won't, succeed," not being afraid of failure, loving people for who they are, and not judging because we are all on this journey together. If one hurts, we all hurt.

Grand-motherhood has given me a 2nd chance to mother. My creativity, care giving, compassion, desire for adventure and travel, and spirituality are traits that I pass on to you, stressing the importance of history in all our relationships. May I always be a good model.

Love,
Mom

Denise L. Scotch

Denise L. Scotch
I was born with the last name of Arendas; I was raised in Twinsburg, Ohio. I raised my family for the last 24 years in Brunswick, Ohio. I am a Travel Coordinator for an insurance company. My BEST and most SATISFYING job has been a Mother for 30 years!

To my daughter, Erin Lynn and my son, Steven John,

Know that: I have to start by saying that my heart is filled with love and joy for both of you! I am very proud of the adults you have grown to be! You both have accomplished things I only dreamed of. Watching each of you graduate from College was two of the happiest of days of my life! That is besides the days you were born February 2 and February 3, five years apart!

The top values I encourage for you are:

FAMILY
Ours is a broken family after 18 years; the divorce was difficult for all of us to adjust. Erin, you were going off to college and, Steven, you were just entering your teens. I was struggling to find my way with everything. As your mother I tried to be the best mother that I could possibly be for you both. Through it all I always tried to instill in you both how important Family is no matter what. I can see now how you both look out for each other. It makes me smile knowing that, Erin, some day you will be a loving and caring Mother and, Steven, you will be a loving Father who is a wonderful provider for his family. You both stood up for me when I married again and have been accepting of our family now. I thank you for your love and support always!

GOALS

I have always encouraged you both to set goals and work toward them. You each have been very successful in surpassing your goals you have set for yourselves in life. Erin, you have exceeded all of my expectations with your job and work ethics in your sales and Associate Manager position. You will soon have the loving marriage, home and family that you always dreamed of. Steven, you have surpassed every goal you have set for yourself in spite of the challenges you have been faced with. They have only made you stronger and more determined in life. You finished college in 3 ½ years, cycling 100 miles in your first race Pelotonia and with only four months of training, not to mention being a Bank Manager too.

MY LEGACY – (MY CHILDREN)

Know that as your Mother I tried very hard to instill in each of you Unconditional Love, Happiness for Life, Laughter, Adventure of Traveling, Positivity, Manners, Respect for Others, and Respect for Yourselves and Wisdom to know what is right. You both are my success in life!

Erin, you were always my challenge as a mom. Yes, I was strict but I had to be. You are a strong and independent, beautiful woman. My prayer for you is to have a daughter as strong and independent as you. You will instinctively know how to raise her!

Steven, you are my motivation in life. You inspire and amaze me in ways I never thought possible. You're strong and independent and handsome. I see the man you are and know in my heart you can deal with anything! Have faith in God, trust in Him, and don't ever give up on yourself.

I Thank God for you both every day of my life! All my love forever......Mom xoxo

Diane Sidoti

I am a Telecommunication Specialist for a packaging manufacturing plant. I have been in the field of Telecom for almost 30 years and the advancements are constant. But being a wife, mother and grandmother have been my most precious privileges in life.

To my 2 sons, Brian and Scott, and my daughter, Kerianne,

How do I possibly explain the ever-changing feelings of being your mother: from the excitement of your birth, to watching all your "firsts," seeing how your environment away from home changed you, but we all still stayed grounded together? And now, seeing the adults that you have become, I look back wondering how did you ever get to be the accomplished people that you are today? Your dad and I were always amazed at all your achievements that started so young and just kept building. Amazement is what I feel the most. You are all a gift that needed nurturing for such a short time – and you grew so quickly into who you are.

Know that: From your first breath to this moment of distance between us you are the most important pieces of my life and you are loved unconditionally. The miles and activities that keep us apart will never change the love, concern and interest in your well-being - be it mentally, emotionally, physically and spiritually. There is nothing that can change the constant in my love for each of you.

The top values I encourage for you are:

MY BEST
Know that I have always tried to do my best for you. Through the stress of our challenging life with your dad's illness, I struggled to juggle relationships of who was the most needy at the time. I wanted you to have as normal

a life as possible under the situation and felt that your dad's strength of character gave you all the example to strive for the top in whatever you went after in life. I too learned from his strengths throughout our marriage, and I hope you weren't too bruised along the way. Only through the Grace of God did we survive intact.

LOOKING FORWARD

I believe our past influences who we are, but it's the moving forward in life that keeps us strong, agile and positive. Have a grateful heart, thanking God daily for His many blessings; keep a positive attitude for smiling will lighten your heart; and find the Jesus in everyone you meet along the way doing your best to give back during your journey of life. Hang on to good friends who know you well enough to help during pain and celebrate during times of joy – yes, celebrate!

Each of you have chosen awesome partners to enrich your lives so beautifully – to Jacque and Sonja a sincere Thank You for being so compassionate and understanding of my sons' needs, desires to achieve, and their love for fun. Thank you for such beautiful grandchildren who are the ultimate joy in my life. To Joseph, Benjamin, Matthew, Sienna and Colt: Be loving and kind always, be honest and fair, and always try your hardest to be the best you can be. To Evan, thank you for enriching Kerianne's life more than we ever thought possible.

I love you all and to partially quote a very wise woman – "Never forget: it's not the finish line but the race by which we are remembered."

Donna Speigel

Nationally recognized as a leader in the resale industry with over 33 years in business, Donna Speigel is President of the Snooty Fox – also a proud member of the Association of Resale Innovation –
In 2006, Donna was honored to be named one the YWCA "CAREER WOMEN OF ACHIEVEMENT".
Most important to Donna and her husband Dennis is their 10 year old grandson Dayton. The Speigels have established the Conductive Learning Center of Greater Cincinnati to benefit children with Cerebral Palsy, Spina Bifida and other motor challenges.

To my children, Jamie, Austin and Taylor, who I love with all my heart, and my beloved grandchildren, Blake, Spencer and Brailynn: my prayers are that you will show your true character, strength, and most of all, love, and help to see Dayton through his life with your presence and that he will continue to be loved and progress in a safe environment.   My hope for all of you is that you make the right, positive decisions and will understand that you get out of life what you put into it.

To my grandson Dayton: I have always wanted to write a book about you, and so here is my own page. I have been so blessed that you came into our lives ten years ago, and we find ourselves raising you, our angel. Dayton, you were diagnosed with Angelman Syndrome, a rare genetic disorder that left you with the beautiful characteristic of always staying happy. You have balance issues, but have worked really hard and have kept progressing. You sat up at two and walked at seven. You are also nonverbal, but you have an excellent way of communicating with your papa and me and all those who are close to you. You are definitely the boss, and we never wonder what you want, whether you are hungry or tired or want to watch one of your favorite cartoon channels.

You are an inspiration to all that you meet: your family, friends, and strangers. You encourage faith in others. Only you could decide to walk your longest walk at Vacation Bible School in front of the entire congregation, down the center aisle, right to the pastor. All of a sudden that day you had gotten away from us, letting go of my hand at the back of the church and walking from the back to the front. There wasn't a dry eye anywhere. This was the miracle of the summer. Of course, there was a lot of hard work behind it, but you chose that moment to walk all the way down and come back to us, giving everyone something like an Obama wave, waving and smiling to this side of the church and then to the other side.

You show no judgment on anyone that you meet. In your eyes everyone is equal. Even Mickey Mouse, whose job is to bring joy to others around the world, was brought to tears meeting you. He followed us out of the Meet-and-Greet Area for an extra hug, and Mickey had to take a break behind the curtain because he was simply brought to tears. The staff there is allowed to make efforts and put money towards making a child's wish come true. The next night when we got back to the room, we saw stuffed animals in the room having a birthday party--with balloons and a blanket and everything imaginable from the Disney gift shop spilling out of the room! What a complete surprise! Each year we go to visit, and you continue to have the same effect on the characters and the people there.

You must continue to try new challenges whether it is going down the stairs, which you can master when you wish to do it, or swimming, or speaking. We are all so proud of you each and every day for your accomplishments at school and at home. You certainly changed the course of our lives, for Papa and me. We didn't picture this for our retirement; actually we never would have, but you, our Angel, came along and showed us the way to the true meaning of life. The reason that our businesses have been successful--there are many reasons-- but we were shown the "why" through you. You inspired us to be more than we were by our opening of the Learning Center in Greater Cincinnati.

Dayton, know that Papa and I are always with you. God has you in His hands and always will. After all, you are truly one of His angels.

With all my Love, Mom

For more info - See appendix

Suzanne Stamper

Suzanne Stamper (nee Greer)
Birth year: 1944
Education: York University, Toronto Canada
Child and Family Studies
Non Profit Sector Administration
Career: Director of a Children's Mental Health Treatment Center
Administrator of a Provincial Mental Health Association
Elected Municipal Councilor
Hobbies: Gardening, decorating, reading, traveling and community volunteerism.

To my son David,

Know that: I wasn't really ready to have a child. I was very career oriented and quite petrified to learn I was pregnant. Would I be a good mother? Would you be healthy? - How would I continue to work and earn my degree? And then you were born, and I held you in my arms. You were perfect; you clutched my finger and my heart melted. Your name "David" means "beloved" and you truly are. You have become a wonderful, caring, loving son, husband and father. I feel so blessed.

The top values I encourage for you are:

LOVE
Love yourself, for it is only through self-love that you can truly love others.

YOUR CHILDREN
Value and cherish the gift that is your children. You already do this so well, David. As a stay-at-home dad, you show my grandchildren, patience, caring, playfulness, wisdom and love.

DIVERSITY
Accept and respect the differences in others. It is only through this value that our home, our community, our country and our world can become whole.

ENJOY LIFE
It is such a cliché but as I get older I see so many people working to accumulate more: a bigger house, a better car, to make more money. Don't forget to laugh, to stand in awe of nature, to roll in the leaves with your children, to appreciate and value the smell of spring, the first snowfall, the tinkling brook, the smile of joy on your child's face.

BE GENEROUS
We all need to give more, to care for others, to give not just monetarily but of our time, our knowledge and our skills. Each of us can remember an act of kindness from our past that we will never forget.

My Wish for you is:
David, you embody all of these attributes and I wish for you, my beautiful daughter-law, and my grandchildren a future full of hope, of peace, of safety, of security and most of all of love.

" What lies behind us and what lies before us are tiny matters compared to what lies within us" - EMERSON

Love Always,
Your Mom

A THOUGHT FROM THE MOM'S CORNER
"The natural state of motherhood is unselfishness. When you become a mother, you are no longer the center of your own universe. You relinquish that position to your children."

Jessica Lange

Leigh B. Taylor

Leigh B. Taylor is an award-winning photographer based in Cincinnati, Ohio. For the past 10 years, she has photographed everything from backyard baseball games to Presidential campaigns, and everything in between.

Leigh grew up in Cincinnati, and knows its unique personality. She has worked for the past 10 years as a staff photographer at the Cincinnati Enquirer, a position that she dreamed of getting as a child. Her job is to tell people's stories through photographs. In addition to her work appearing in the local newspaper, she has also photographed for national publications. Leigh studied Broadcasting at Marquette University for a Bachelors degree, and also earned a masters degree in Visual Communications from Ohio University's renowned School of Visual Communication.

She is a mother to two wonderful children, Jake, 4, and Evie, 2.

To my son Jake and daughter Evie,

Know that: It seems like yesterday that we brought you two home. Even though you came to us in different ways, you are both my little miracles.

With you Jake, my labor was physically painful, though it brought tears of joy to my eyes when you were born. I loved watching your Daddy rock and whisper to you when you were only a few minutes old. The first few months were exhausting, and I wondered how we would make it with such little sleep. However, your first smile lit up the room, and I never loved you more.

I had a different kind of "labor" with you, Evie. At 10 months old, I held you close as you cried and asked for your foster mother on the plane ride home from South Korea. I remember you would calm down momentarily, then look up at my face and burst into tears again because you didn't know who I was. It was an emotionally exhausting 24 hours, but I'm so glad that I was the one who was able to comfort you. Only a week or so later, I was the face that you were looking for. I'll never forget when you gave us your first smile while swinging in the backyard on your third day home. As soon as we received your photo when you were just one month old, we fell in love with you.

Right now you are 2 and 4 years old, and are happy with each other. My favorite thing to do is to watch you play and laugh together. The other day you both were picking flowers and Jake held out his bouquet for Evie to smell. It was such a simple, yet sweet moment. And of course I captured it on film. I can't wait to experience more moments.

The top values I encourage for you are:

GREAT MEMORIES AND BEST EDUCATION
I want you both to have great memories of your childhood and get the best education that we can provide.

BE RESPONSIBLE AND GIVING
I wish that you both grow up to be responsible and loving adults, and most of all to be "people for others." My parents and teachers taught me the value of being socially responsible and giving back to others, and I hope to teach the same thing to you both.

BE OPEN TO NEW EXPERIENCES
Have big hearts, and open yourselves up to new experiences. Remember that life is short, and live life to the fullest.

I couldn't be more proud of the two of you, Jake and Evie. Always remember that you are loved.
Mom

Jennifer Teipel

Jennifer Teipel is the Executive Director for Campbell County Media Central where she provides instruction in television production to students, not-for-profit organizations and community members as well as negotiates and regulates cable franchise documents. She has produced award-winning cable television programming, served on the Central States Alliance for Community Media, Executive Produced the Blue Chip Cable Access Awards, and serves on the Campbell County Drug Free Coalition. For volunteer activities, Jennifer serves on the Jolly Park Community Development Council and also serves on the Administrative Council for her church. She received her Bachelor of Arts in Radio/Television/Film from Northern Kentucky University. Jennifer enjoys running, kayaking, hiking, playing piano and the flute, vacationing at the beach and most importantly, enjoys being with her family.

To my sweet, beautiful, bright and talented daughter, Kara (14),

Know that: When God blessed me with you, my most precious gift, my life was forever changed. You fill my heart so full of joy it sometimes overwhelms me with emotion. You bring so much to my life: Laughter, with that witty sense of humor, pride, as I witness all of your accomplishments and hope, as I think about what gifts you bring to this world and what life has in store for you. I love you more than you can possibly imagine.

The top values I encourage for you are:

KEEP FAITH AS PRIORITY IN YOUR LIFE
My faith has been one of the things that has sustained me throughout some of the biggest challenges in my life. Knowing God is with you and carrying you through obstacles will give you the strength to persevere through all of life's challenges. Faith will also help you celebrate the blissful moments in your life.

LOVE

Love is unconditional. Settle for nothing less when choosing whom to spend your life with. As your mother, no words can begin to describe how much love I have for you. Our family, and our love for one another, makes my life complete. My dream for you is that you will live life with a heart always filled with love.

RESPECT

Respect life, nature's beauty and others. When you treat your life, as well as other people, with respect, they will share a respect for you. Respect life and the beautiful world around it. Enjoy nature's beauty and have respect for it so it stays that way.

HAPPINESS

Success should not be measured by wealth and fortune. God has BIG plans for you. Success IS finding and following that purpose. You will find true happiness in life by measuring your successes with the things in life that REALLY matter. Work hard for those things. In there, you will find true happiness.

MUSIC

Music can be very therapeutic, whether you are listening to it or making it. Continue with the talent you were given, whether you play simply for your own pleasure, or for others. Musical ability stays with you your whole life. It is a beautiful gift.

THE MOST IMPORTANT ADVICE I WANT TO GIVE TO YOU

Live and enjoy all the moments in your life. Make sure that you take time to appreciate every moment in life as you are living it, and always remember that you are the sparkle in my life!

I will love you always, Mom

Janie Telljohann

Janie Telljohann
Master's of Education (Intervention)
Classroom teacher 2 ½ years, Home
school tutor 1 year
Married to Michael for 6 happy years!
Hobbies: reading, cooking, making
jewelry, crafts, and traveling

To my daughters - Sara and Katherine and my stepsons – Brian and Brandon, all between 21 – 25 years old,

ALWAYS GIVE MORE THAN YOU GET IN RETURN
Giving has always been big in my life. Even when I was divorced and a single Mom, I always gave to people less fortunate than us. I still do this with various volunteering and activities. It really is true that you get back double or more when you give to someone else.

APPRECIATION
Always write Thank You notes to people who give you gifts or call people to thank them for thinking about you. A handwritten note is the best and every gift is worthy of a thank you. Take the time to write because they spent time shopping for that "special gift." Always appreciate the thought rather than the gift itself.

GRANDPARENTS / FAMILY
I have the best memories of spending summers or breaks with my grandparents. They would let me set up house on their front porch or play in the basement. I also remember walking to the store with my grandmother because she didn't drive. When I could drive, I would take her myself. I remember great sleepovers, even when I was a teenager. You can learn lots of valuable history about the family and also about that special someone. I am not a grandparent right now but plan to be that fun grandparent that I once had! I was close to my Dad and

he always had that" gift" of knowing everyone even complete strangers.

TRAVEL

I have always had the wanderlust of visiting different places. I feel that life is too short and eating/traveling the world is the best. There is so much beauty and we miss so much by not traveling. I have tried to take you to places to have that experience. Never stop looking and experiencing!

KNOWLEDGE

I went back to college in my late 40's and was very glad to be able to expand my knowledge. I was able to teach students with disabilities and have left classroom to tutor. I love to pass my knowledge and my love of reading to my students. We never stop learning!

RESPONSIBILITY

Take responsibility for things you want to accomplish. Whether it is your career, family, or travels, all this is your responsibility. I hopefully gave you the tools and you will need to use them.

PARENTING

Being a parent was a scary job and also a very fun job. I was able to stay home and really spend time with my children. I would never trade any job or career for the precious time we spent together. I never believed time would have gone so quickly, but it is true that your children grow up fast. Treasure the play time, bath time, reading before bed, making up stories, and just experiencing the little joys of being a parent.

I have always stressed to my daughters that you can do and be anything (career wise) that you want to be. I changed mine several times but always enjoyed being a Mom. I sat at all the dance recitals, sports, and any other events with the proud Mom smile. I still am very proud of all that the both of you have accomplished. You still have so much more to gain through your life experiences. Just remember, I love you both and will always be proud. Pass life on in any way you can! Give of yourself!

Love, Mommy

Aymsley Toomer

Aymsley Toomer
Born: Mobile, Alabama
BA: Marymount College
Marketing Manager for Prasco Laboratories
Married 30 years to Jack Atherton
Two Daughters:
Gray 25 (Graduate School, University of Houston)
Chase 20 (Brasenose College, Oxford University)

Best talent: Creole cooking from my Louisiana mother

To my Daughters Chase and Gray,

Know that:
I stumbled into motherhood with the naiveté that comes from being raised by two wonderful parents who loved my sister and me and sacrificed to give us the best life they could imagine. I had no doubt that I would be able to do the same. Being a mother comes naturally, doesn't it? I could not have been more wrong.

Another misguided assumption was that it would be my job to teach you how to be good wives and mothers; but in reality, it was your dad who taught me how to be a wife and you two who taught me how to be a mother. Dad and I were married five years before we became parents. I was 36 when you, Gray, were born and 41 when you, Chase, came into the world. You were healthy, beautiful-- and even when you were toddlers--hilarious. Some of the happiest memories I have are of our family just doing ordinary things together like feeding the ducks or hiking in Sharon Woods.

We decided that the best start was for one of us to stay home while you were small. I was grateful that Dad was willing to shoulder the responsibility of keeping us afloat financially, but it was truly a life lesson in living within your means. Financial worries can take a toll on your marriage. For our anniversary celebration your dad bought stick-on stars that glowed in the dark and put them on the ceiling in our bedroom. His card was a take-off on an Oscar Wilde line, "We may end up in the gutter but we will always have the stars." His wit and dark humor have carried us over many bumps in the road. Between breast-feeding, changing diapers, keeping the house clean and grocery shopping, I could barely keep my head above water. I had grown up in a house but had never run a house. Dad knew less than I did.

Not that there weren't rewards that can only be described as miraculous. At six months you, Gray, would sit on my stomach as I stretched out on the bed and we would talk. You would gibber back, imitating some of the sounds you heard and as time went on your conversation matured into real words. You have remained gregarious to this day, and a dead-on mimic. It is a gift.

Chase, you were completely different-- serious and shy but with a will of iron. Although separated by five years you never considered yourself any less than your big sister's complete equal. On arriving at Gray's first sleepover, you struggled to get out of your car seat. It was explained that these were your sister's friends and older. You tearfully answered, "Yes, but if they knew I was here, they would ask me to stay."

As you both grew up, we did have a few rules: "Please and Thank You," "Please tell me how I can help you, not what your problem is," "I can't hear you when you whine," "You are not allowed to use 'bad words,' call someone 'stupid,' or a 'liar,'" "No television or games until your homework is complete," and finally, "Something may be true, but if it is also mean and hurtful...it's best left unsaid." These rules worked most of the time.

More than twenty years have passed since Chase was born and though both of you are far away studying—I have never felt more the immediacy of motherhood. There is such a history—so many good times and some scary bad times, too—that we are bound forever by our understanding and acceptance of each other.

I am so grateful that I was given your two little souls to care for and will love you both completely until my last dying breath.   All My Love, Mom

Anne Valyo

Anne Valyo was born in Edinburgh, Scotland and now lives in Brechin. Her late husband, Jim, was originally from Ohio but spent much of his life in the UK working for the US government. Anne has been a teacher, singer and actor and is now a lecturer of Drama/Theatre in the University of Aberdeen. She lives with her younger son, Wesley, and younger daughter,Natasha, but makes regular visits to her son, Neil and daughter-in-law, Rona, and their two girls, Lily and Mary and to her daughter, Nicola and son-in-law, Paul, and their two boys, Lucas and Oliver and their baby girl, Anya, who live respectively in Haddington, near Edinburgh and Newbury Park, near Los Angleles!!

To my children, Neil, Nicola, Wesley and Natasha,

Know that: I love you all, totally and unconditionally, as only a parent can do. Make that your bedrock for all time. It will be a strong, sure foundation for all your life because that love will never die. Always know that you are loved no matter the distance we are apart, how long we are apart or even if death should part us.

As Shakespeare in his sonnet No. 116 states,
"Love is not love
Which alters when it alteration finds,...,
O no! It is an ever-fixed mark
That looks on tempests and is never shaken;
It is the star to every wandering bark,"
I have always known my parents' love. They have now gone, but their love remains and keeps me strong even to this day.

MAKING MISTAKES
As your mother, I try my hardest to be the best mother I can be for you. There are days when I do everything reasonably well and go to bed happy, but there are other days when I make so many mistakes I think I should have stayed in bed as I must be the worst mother on the planet!
Actually, making mistakes is good. You learn from your mistakes not your successes. So don't beat yourself up

about your mistakes because, as Alexander Pope wrote, *"To err is human, to forgive, divine."* Hopefully you will not make the same mistakes twice – you will just make different ones! And, please, learn to forgive yourself.

LIFE'S OPPORTUNITIES
Be open to adventures! If a door opens for you, go through it and experience what is beyond it. If there is a closed door which looks intriguing, hammer on it till it opens for you. Remember, nothing is impossible. Above all, follow your dreams and your heart for then you will find happiness.

FUN
Try to find time in your busy lives for fun. Do something you really enjoy at least once a week!

BEING POSITIVE
Try to do one good thing each day. It may be helping someone else, calling an old friend, or even just paying a bill. Then at the end of the day you can look back and be happy that you have done something positive.

FRIENDS
Try to keep in touch with friends from school, college, work, etc. I know you have your families but friends are important too. Unlike family, friends are with you through choice!

LIFE'S GOOD TIMES
I like to remember the good times and imagine that I could save them forever in a bubble or a pod that would never burst. Pod moments can then be remembered whenever I feel sad. Instantly they bring a smile to my face again, letting me re-live that particularly joyful moment in time. I hope you all have loads of "pod moments" in your lives!

Finally, be thankful for each and every day you have on this earth.

All my love, Mum xxxxxxx

Joann Ward

Joann Ward (nee Zdinak) Born 1981
Married to Andy Ward for 3.5 years
2004 – ASN From Miami University Ohio
CAREER - Registered Nurse, Worked in
Trauma, Organ Donation, and Diagnostic
Cardiology
Loves Sports, helping others, and
spending time with Friends and family!

To my daughter Sydney (19 months),

Know that: Your father and I have loved you even before we knew you were possible. After a long year and a half we were blessed to find out that you were going to be our child. We knew at 20 weeks that you had my nose and daddy and I got to see your heart beat. I never knew my heart could stop just by watching yours. I didn't know you were a girl, but on the day we had you I listened to the song "Isn't she lovely." As tears rolled down my face I had a feeling it was your way of letting me know. Then you came into this world and we found out what you already "told" me, you were our baby girl. I looked at you and remembered every part of your face. As we have watched you grow we talk to you about what you will be when you grow up but know you will do great in whatever you choose. From your first smile, step, and word you make us feel whole. The songs you sing everyday make my heart smile and I love being your mommy. To walk through the door and see your unconditional love every day is something you give me without even trying. My wish for you one day is to realize you are special and loved by everyone in your life. I look forward to all of your milestones and sharing them with you. Every day I am honored to be your mother.

The top values I encourage for you are:

DO WHAT MAKES YOU HAPPY
As you grow up, you will hear what you "should" do a lot.

Remember you write your own book and what seems to be right for others may not be right for you. You will learn from your mistakes and will make your own right way in life. I will be there to support you and pick you up when you fall and help you on your journey. You may find that your mistakes weren't that at all; they were things that just happened before you knew they could help you.

BE YOUR OWN ME
Not everyone will know you until you choose to show them you. Be yourself and if you are meant to have them in your life, they will be there. It is much harder to keep trying to be who someone wants you to be. You never go wrong when you just be you.

BE ENCOURAGING AND YOU WILL BE ENCOURAGED
"Do unto others" is not just a figure of speech. If you give others what you would want for yourself, you will find you surround yourself with people that do the same. Encouragement is a strong and powerful tool.

WHEN YOU ARE DOWN TALK TO PEOPLE
Life isn't always out to get you. You will ALWAYS find people that have it worse, and it is what they choose to let pull them down that make them who they are. Even if at the time you feel like it can't get any worse, talk to people around you and learn that sometimes by helping others you help yourself.

FAMILY NEVER GOES AWAY
You may not like each other all the time but know that no matter what, you are family and they will be there for you. You will look back and remember bad times, but the good times will always be the times you don't need to remember for you just know those times.

I Love you in every way, Mommy

Lois Wegman

Lois (Donelan) Weghorn
Born 1946 –
Married to Paul Weghorn for 43 years –
Graduate of:
Our Lady of Providence 1964 –
Walmart Employee – 19 years
Enjoys yard work and traveling –
especially to the Smokey Mountains with
the family

To my five outstanding sons, Rick 40, Rob 37, Steve 34, Jason and Dave 31. To my wonderful grandchildren Riley, Ryan, Ella, Gage, Lacy, and all future grandchildren,

Know that: Loving all of you has been and always will be the greatest priority in our life. All of us have become better people working together as a family. Your dad and I are so proud of all your accomplishments. You have enriched and blessed our lives with joy and love. We love you unconditionally. We wish you all the best with your wonderful families.

The top values I encourage for you are:

DO THE RIGHT THING
My hope for all of you is to continue your belief in God. Pray often for guidance, forgiveness and strength. God will always be there in your most difficult times. Actions and words are important to the people you will meet in your life. Treat them as you would like to be treated. They are all part of God's family. People will try to influence your decisions, but do the right thing for yourself and your family.

FAMILY
Our love of family will always bond us together whether we are far away or nearby. As individuals you have your own ideas and goals. But as a family we have strived to

help make our lives better for those we love. Stay close; you will grow with a deeper appreciation for each other.

SET A GOOD EXAMPLE
Your children that you have now, and those coming in the future, will follow your example. Help them to be positive and happy. They will pick up and follow things that you say and do. Be a good listener; you will learn from them. When mistakes are made, help your children to accept responsibility for their actions. Saying "I'm sorry" is hard for all of us. Holding anger and bitterness is not healthy for them or your family. They may be young but treating people with respect and dignity is something they will learn from you. Hugs, kisses, and laughter are priceless.

SERVICE TO THE COMMUNITY
Making a difference in people's lives is something all of you have accomplished. As past and present members of our local Fire Department (Central Campbell), you have all served our community. Whenever the tones sounded, whether fire or squad, there is no greater joy in my heart than to know you are there to lend a helping hand. With respect and a sincere sense of duty, you have helped people at their most difficult times. Sometimes a caring smile or a reassuring voice will bring comfort to a worried patient. God bless all of you for your dedicated service.

BE CHEERFUL
Smiling and being cheerful is a contagious quality. People will respond to you even if their day is not so pleasant. Look for the good in them. Your example may be just what they need.

PRAY OFTEN
Pray often for God's love and protection. Be patient and forgiving when necessary. Share your wonderful sense of humor and talents. Time waits for no one. Live life to the fullest.

Bless you and all my love, Mom/Grandma

Melissa Wiley

Melissa Wiley
Education: Milford High School,
University of Cincinnati: Accounting,
CPA
Career: Deloitte & Touche, Uptown
Rental Properties
Hobbies: Half Marathons, Travel,
Cooking

To my beautiful children, Kayla (of age 13), Nicholas (of age 11), and Nathan (of age 9)

Know that: Being your mom is a blessing.

What a joy and privledge it is to have you as my children and to be a mom. I remember my mother-in-law telling me many times, "Children grow up so fast". And now, as I look back over the last 13 years of being a mom, I completely agree, children grow-up **too** fast. Every stage of your lives has brought new challenges and new rewards. Some days and weeks may have seemed almost endless with the challenges of raising three little kids. I remember practically wishing some of those earlier days away. I looked forward to the day when you would sleep through the night or when you would finally be out of diapers and using the potty. I also remember the rewards I have experienced as a mom. I remember the joy of your first steps, the excitement of the first day of school, and the pride I felt when you scored your first goal in soccer. It seems impossible to believe that 13 years have passed and that Kayla, the first born, only has a little over 4 years left before she leaves our nest.This reminds me how important it is to enjoy our times together and embrace my role as a mother.

The top values I encourage for you are:

DO YOUR BEST
Be the best version of yourselves that you can be. Perfection is not the goal; putting forth personal best effort is.

CELEBRATE YOUR UNIQUENESS
Each of you is unique and special and I will always support you and help you achieve your individual goals.

BE GUIDED BY HIGH MORAL CHOICES
Treat others with kindness and generosity. Follow your principles of knowing right from wrong. Love and revere God.

KNOW YOU ARE LOVED
Know that I love you greatly and that my love is unconditional. I try to show this through both my words and my actions. Each night, as I kiss you goodnight, I tell you of my love for you. I want you to know that if you should fall, I will always be there to pick you up. I try to show you that you are loved by spending time with you, talking to you, and listening to you. I love being your mom and I am so blessed to have you as my children.

Love, your mom

Karen Hellyer Wojciechowski

Karen Hellyer Wojciechowski
Born 1975
Married to Paul for 5 years
1997 - AS, Applied Science, University Of Cincinnati
2000 - BS, Construction Management, University of Cincinnati
CAREER - Construction management, Child Care Aide, and best title of all- Mother
HOBBIES – Kids, kids, kids! God, Family, sports, the great outdoors, anything fun!

To my shining stars: My son Ivan age 4, my daughter Meeka age 2, and to your unborn angel siblings,

"Before you were conceived I wanted you. Before you were born I loved you. Before you were here an hour I would give my life for you. This is the miracle of life."
-   Maureen Hawkins

Know that: The Love of a parent to a child is indefinable. No Love can be stronger, bigger, as boundless, deep, infinite, and utterly inexplicable.

From the moment you were placed in my belly, your Dad and my life changed in the best way imaginable. We are dedicated to you and so proud of you. We will love you and protect you forever.

Thank you to the author for allowing me my chance to formally attempt to express a smidge of my Love and to share a secret with my kids...Do you think big tough dads do not cry? Wrong! Overwhelmed with Love for you, Daddy cried at the moments you entered this world.

The top values I encourage for you are:

FAMILY AND GRATITUDE
Be loving and caring to each other. Siblings are irreplaceable. Your sister/brother will always be there for you and love you. Family is the most important.

Be kind to everyone. Be polite. Be respectful. Be honest.
Be thankful. Be generous. Live a healthy lifestyle and
have high morals. Keep your innocence. Be proud of
yourself, your country and your faith. Thank The Lord
every chance you get.

SEIZE THE DAY AND BE POSITIVE

True happiness exists within your own heart. You are
responsible for deciding to be happy. Each day in life is a
gift. Try your best to remember that, especially on really
bad days. There truly is a reason for everything that
happens in life, even if you do not see it at the moment.
Life lessons make you stronger and smarter. Surround
yourself with positive people and be a positive person.
Pray hard. God will answer in His own way.

BELIEVE AND ACHIEVE

I wish for you a long, joyful, active life, full of happiness,
Love and patience. Be a leader. Show confidence.
Always do the right thing. Life is a challenge and a
competition. Yes, there are winners and losers. Your
best fighting chance at success is a high quality
education. Do your best. Try with 110 percent effort at
all you do. Believe in yourself and you will accomplish
your dreams.

REMEMBER

You make me happy. You are my world. You will always
be my precious babies even when you are grown. Come
home anytime. Ivan and Meeka, and Angels above,
together you are my sunshine. I Love you infinity times
infinity. Never forget.

Come home and I'll throw the biggest party heaven has
ever seen   - Luke 15:7

With All my Heart & Soul, I Love You, Mommy

Nancy Ross Zimmerman

Nancy Ross Zimmerman
Born: Cincinnati, Ohio
BM: Westminster Choir College,
Princeton, NJ
MDiv: Louisville Presbyterian
Theological Seminary
Married 17 years to Craig Zimmerman.
First husband, Jeff Ross died in 1989.
Three Children:
Rob Ross, 32 (married to Debbie,
children: Tennyson and Delaney)
Jessica Zimmerman, 27
(married to Michael)
Ashley Ross, 26
Best talent: loves singing with children
and meeting new friends

To my children, Robert, Jessica, and Ashley (ages 26-32) who have been my joy and treasure,

Know that: I always wanted to be a mom. Even before I was married I had selected names for three girls and three boys!

When I was engaged to marry your dad, my minister's wife wrote me a lovely letter of congratulations on our engagement. She shared her belief that being a mother would be the most important role I would ever have. She even included a mathematical equation showing the number of lives impacted by two strong, faithful children who would then raise two strong, faithful children, etc. It was obvious that because of the way I intentionally raised my children, I could have a tremendous impact on the world. Mrs. Maude wrote: "Nancy, the job of being a mom is the most important job you will ever have. No matter how wonderful your career may be, the legacy you can leave as a good mom will far outweigh any career." I took that to heart.

The top values I encourage for you are:

THREE IMPORTANT WORDS
When you were toddlers, we began working together on reading. The first three flash cards I made for you were "look," "see," and "play."
Now that Rob is a dad and has children, I have made Tennyson and Delaney their first set of flash cards which include "look," "see," and "play." Those three words have been so important to me! **LOOK** and **SEE** what is around you and appreciate what is there every day, and then **PLAY** - enjoy life.

LEARN TO FIND HAPPINESS
As a family, we have learned that while money can make you comfortable, it cannot make you happy. The significant relationships in life are essential to maintain and nurture. Ultimately, your happiness will grow from your right relationships. Keep in touch with your siblings!!

UNDERSTAND YOUR PRIORITIES
At Rob's high school graduation ceremony, I appreciated the illustration about priorities in life. The image was of trying to fill a jar with rocks of assorted sizes. You've got to put the biggest rocks in first. Then all the little rocks fill in the cracks. I've tried to help you see the biggest rocks are your relationship with God and your love for family. Career, hobbies, friendships can all fall into place.

DISCOVER YOUR PASSION AND PURSUE IT
Discover what makes your heart glad (those are your strengths!), and find a way to use those things to make the world a better place.

IF YOU ARE IN DOUBT – DON'T
Mom's final word of wisdom: When in doubt, don't!

Love, Mom

Appendix
Donna Speigel

Dayton is truly a beautiful child. You should see this little guy. His eyes look at you, and he takes his little hand and he touches your cheek, and it is just like the world stops. He is just mesmerizing and he is beautiful; he really is. I think this is a part of his gift to be so beautiful--every little curl on his head and his beautiful little face. People are just drawn to him and are drawn in. He puts you into a different state of mind. People in the mall that don't even know him are drawn in. He tweaks his nose to say, "I like you." Or "I like this new toy." Or "Papa's home." So we say that just tweaking your nose is his way of saying, "Hello" to anybody. I have seen people at Kroger tweaking their noses at him. And why wouldn't you do it in response to a child? The kids at school who are verbal sometimes tweak their noses too. If Dayton is acting upset, for instance, or isn't eating his lunch, they too might tweak their noses. They know how Dayton talks. Like the little boy named Preston, if Dayton is not eating his food or something, Preston will tweak his nose and say "Uh, oh, Dayton, eat your lunch." That is how the children check up on each other. Dayton has only a fifteen word vocabulary, but I haven't' given up. We were told that he wouldn't even walk, but he has done that and so much more now.

Proudly, the Speigels have established the Conductive Learning Center of Greater Cincinnati to benefit children with Cerebral Palsy, Spina Bifida and other motor challenges. The Snooty Fox is the main benefactor of the learning center, through their non-profit arm Angel Fox.

For more information visit:
www.shopsnooty.com
www.clcgc.org

CONCLUSION

This book presents many different viewpoints from mothers who share their insights, struggles, values and priorities. Their emphases may be different, but they are all focused on being good mothers to their children. Sometimes it's not the message – but who delivers it, when it is delivered, and how it is delivered.

As your children read this book – be patient. Only some of what they read may be absorbed right now, but it is in writing. Keep this book open and visible. Chances are they will come back to it from time to time. It's a reference book on life.

I encourage you to talk to your children and be patient with them. Continue to look for different ways to get your message across to them- write to them if need be. Keep your doors of communication open - choose your battles very – very – very carefully. Never lose sight of your priorities and keep you lives in balance so your ride in life will be smooth.

Continue to do the next right thing...Then the next...Then the next.

Best,

R. K. Ketterer

Complimentary PDF Copy
(From The Dad's Corner / From The Mom's Corner)

What started out to be a rather small project, specifically for my own two daughters, grew to be something significantly larger. As fathers and mothers became aware of this concept and process, they were excited and energized by it. From there it grew – and grew exponentially.

Now I have come to realize how important and powerful these two books are. I have come to understand that every person who has the status of son or daughter can learn and benefit from these books. I've broadened my focus to other children – especially children who do not necessarily have a mother's or father's positive influence in their lives.

There are many young people who could greatly benefit from these books since they offer such a strong influence in living positive, constructive lives.

So I reach out to you for your help – your help to direct a free copy of this book to them.

To request a complimentary PDF version of either book (which can be displayed on most electronic devices), please contact the author by using the information listed on page 146.

(Write Your Own Page)

```
Insert your
photo here &
bio to right
```

To_____

_____,

Know that:_____

_____
_____
_____
_____

The top values I encourage for you are:

_____
_____
_____
_____

_____
_____
_____
_____

_____
_____
_____
_____

_____
_____
_____
_____

QUICK ORDER FORM

Order information

Both books are available at:

www.fromthedadscorner.com

Contact information:

R. K. Ketterer
19 Spillman Drive
Alexandria, KY 41001

Email:
fromthedadscorner@gmail.com

Phone:
859-635-8604

If you would like to submit your page(s) for possible inclusion in upcoming volumes of *From The Dad's Corner* or *From The Mom's Corner* then go to the web site: www.fromthedadscorner.com.

CPSIA information can be obtained at www.ICGtesting.com
Printed in the USA
LVOW11s2011151213

365417LV00001B/1/P